unleashed

GOD'S SPIRIT IS ON THE MOVE IN INDIA

Lessons from an Indigenous Revolution

SAM STEPHENS

Dedication

I'd like to dedicate this book to the thousands of barefoot pastors and to Women with a Mission disciplers who are on the front lines of India Gospel League's work. May God continue to draw you close to himself, to grow you, and to grant you a great harvest in the villages of India.

Contents

Foreword

If I had to select only one global leader to introduce to American church leaders, I would pick Sam Stephens, the author of the book you are about to read. I would not select Sam because he's so impressive; but I would pick Sam because it is so impressive how God has chosen to work through him. I want every leader in the West to see and hear from Sam because he has had the privilege of leading the kind of missional movement that we all work towards and pray for in our context. So, when Sam asked if I would write this foreword in hopes of introducing him to more leaders in the United States and Europe, I quickly said, "Yes!"

I vividly remember the day I was introduced to Sam Stephens. I was hurrying through my day when I looked at my schedule and saw an appointment with a guy named Sam. I asked my assistant, Pat, why I had this meeting and who Sam was. "I thought you knew him," she said. "All I know is that he is from India."

I went into the meeting wondering if this would be a waste of my time. I greeted the man, extended my hand, and asked him to tell me his story. Sam started back in the 1950s, with a story about his father. Sam's father had started a mission to plant churches in India, and he told me by 1992 they had experienced some growth. During that time, they had planted two hundred churches, and all could be traced to that first church started by Sam's dad in the '50s. "Wow," I thought. Two hundred churches! Sam had my attention now.

Sam wasn't comfortable talking about his own work; he's very humble. So, I had to drag the rest of the details out of him. He told me that in 1992, he had taken over the mission, and he made a simple but strategic shift in the way they did things. He began to insist that every church planter not only plant a church but also have an apprentice church planter. This was someone who would come alongside the planter and learn firsthand how to plant a church; this way the reproduction would continue year after year at each church.

Now I was really curious and asked, "How is that going?" Without much expression, Sam replied, "Well, we now have seventy thousand churches." At that point, I was glad that I was sitting down. I was beginning to realize that this was an incredible story. I asked Sam, "How many people does that represent?" And again, his reply took my breath away. "I think about 3.5 million," he said. Then he added, "But we are praying for one hundred thousand churches and 5 million people!"

At that, I began to wonder: how did this kind of multiplication movement happen? In talking further with Sam, I learned that the simple shift he had made back in 1992 had transformed the results of their church-planting efforts. Sam had discovered that there were people and leaders all over India who had gifts, and if he could empower them, encourage them, and commission them, then Jesus' mission would move forward at an exponential rate.

To this day, I'm still not sure how I got that appointment with Sam…but I'm sure glad I did! Since that time, I have been with Sam many times and he has taught me many lessons. But the lessons he teaches are not lessons he got on his own but are rather his observations from working where God is at work. And because he's learned to put his best efforts where God is at work, the India Gospel League has planted and unleashed more than 100,000 churches under his leadership.

If reading *Unleashed* is your introduction to Sam, I am excited for you! If you already know Sam, you've probably skipped this foreword to get on to the good stuff! Sam Stephens is a godly, humble, hero-making leader who is seeing God work in ways that we all long to see happen in the West. He is an important prophetic voice to the Western church. My advice: read this book slowly, lean into every word, listen to what the Spirit is saying to you about how to join the work God is doing to unleash the church.

Dave Ferguson
Lead Pastor – Community Christian Church, Chicago
President – Exponential
Author – *Hero Maker: Five Essential Practices for Leaders to Multiply Leaders*

Introduction

Two decades into the new millennium and, oh, how things have changed. Twenty years ago, I would not have predicted that it would be so dangerous to be a Christian in India. I would not have imagined that the window of opportunity for our Western friends to visit India would close. I would not have guessed that my government would stop Western dollars from supporting the work that we do here.

Sharon Campus has been my home for thirty-five years. It is still a serene and hopeful oasis for the 400 children (mostly orphans) who live and attend school here, for the university students who would have been shut out of a degree if it were not for our community college, for the sick in the care of our hospital staff, and for the special needs children who receive therapy, love, education, and a home.

Today, as I look out my window at this beautiful scene, I am reflecting on all that God has done here. I am meditating on the miracles he has worked through brothers and sisters all across my country. Some of you who have been our friends for a long time know that because of his mighty hand, India Gospel League—our network of church planters and disciplers across India—has planted 100,000 churches since 1992. That's about 99,000 more than we ever thought possible, and a movement of God that I certainly couldn't have predicted.

Over forty years ago, when I was twenty-four, I went out to the villages as a barefoot pastor (or a church planter, you might say), camping out amongst the people and sharing the gospel with those who had never heard. My journey of watching God work in real time began in earnest. I saw firsthand what happens when the darkness is pierced with clarity and when the person of Jesus is truly made known to the lost, the poor, the hungry, the uneducated, the outcast. Today, millions across South Asia still need to hear the Good News about Jesus and experience practical blessings such as education, medical care, and economic opportunity.

The Lord has equipped India Gospel League to train and connect thousands of indigenous barefoot pastors to bring the gospel and its many practical blessings out to the villages. We are seeing hundreds of thousands of Indian people come to the Lord and be established in the word, discipled, raised up, and unleashed to love and serve their neighbors.

Now, we are at a crossroads. Our government is clamping down, making threats, and fomenting violence, but God's Kingdom in India is growing vibrantly, organically, and exponentially.

If you've read my book *The Kairos Moment*, you know that I believe we can see God working in specific ways and at specific times—and that the spiritually discerning believer does not hesitate to join into this work. An absolute work of God is unfolding in India right now. Frankly, not many days go by that I am not thinking about, praying about, dreaming about, and talking about where I believe this work is going. And I believe that in the next twenty years, another unexpected—and perhaps unbelievable—event will come to pass. I believe that we will see all of India reached with the gospel.

Because God has unleashed an equipping, discipling, planting, indigenous church in India, it is not "what if" but "when" will everyone hear the name of Jesus Christ. There are millions here who have never even heard his name. Close to half of all unreached people in the world live in this country. Yet I firmly believe that in the next twenty years, the unleashed indigenous church will have taken the gospel out to every one of our 600,000 villages, where the vast majority of those unreached people live. Keep your eyes peeled and your ears open. Watch, pray, and join in as this miracle unfolds.

Now, my Western friends, I've found that my burden for this miracle in India has been intertwined with a burden for you. Think back twenty years. Could you have predicted the state of the Western church today? American churches are losing their youth, and they may not get them back. Studies conclude that America has already joined Europe as post-Christian.

Western churches have tried to combat this loss by catering to a rotating, ever-more consumer culture in which many are seeking the best worship experience, coffee, and childcare rather than the freedom and joy found in Jesus Christ. The "Nones" are the fastest rising religious demographic. And while you are witnessing the decline of Western Christianity, from my across-the-ocean point of view, I am seeing a declining interest in world missions from the States. I've wondered if these things are connected. Perhaps in a concern for their own local churches, Western believers are turning inward, appropriating an "America first" or "focus on local" model to the body of Christ.

What is happening at this crossroads? Where is God working in the West? What is he doing? Where is he going?

Through visits and conversations with some of you, I've come to believe that at "such a time as this," we Indian believers may have something to share with our Western brothers and sisters. We are watching Christianity ignite and spread across our country—one person at a time, one village at a time. Without any cumbersome traditions or human structures, excited believers, empowered by the Holy Spirit, are boldly sharing their faith. I believe we can show and remind you what it looks like to follow Jesus in this stripped-down way. We are following the Spirit in order to work where God is working. I'd love to offer what we've learned so that you can put it to work in your context.

One of the biggest drivers motivating the underground gospel revolution in India is a recognition that life comes from death and growth comes from giving. The poorest of the poor are offering their last coins to advance the gospel; and they are quite literally giving up their lives for Jesus and the people they love. There is no better way (because it is God's way) for a Christian, for a church, to strengthen what remains than by living this loving, radically other-centered life. If the church in India is ignited by radical other centeredness, then why not the American church as well?

Work where God is working. Grow through giving. This is how we are multiplying in India. I believe that you can apply these principles in your context at home *and* apply them by joining in our work in India. I've attempted to write this book in a practical way so that you're able to take the material and use it to evaluate your own role in the story

God is writing in our world.

Do I believe that your participation in God's work in India can ignite *your* life? Your people's lives? Your church? Absolutely. It is an opportunity which, if taken, will not only connect your people with the unprecedented work of God in India, but will ignite and strengthen hearts for God's work at home. It is an opportunity for all of us.

chapter 1

WHERE IN THE WORLD IS THE CHURCH HEADED?

UNLEASHED

Dear Friend,

We want to take this time to say **THANK YOU** for your prayers and support for children, pastors and families of India.

We continue to keep an eye on the spread of Covid-19 in the West and are continuing to keep you in our prayers.

Amidst a world in complete turmoil, when the new normal seems to be "uncertainty," we believers remain certain of this: *Christ is coming back, and he is building his church.*

I am excited and grateful for the opportunity—right at this moment in history—to share my latest book, *Unleashed.* The **church that Jesus is building** is not a structure, not a fortress, and not an institution. It is a force with which to be reckoned, *a wave of love; it is an unleashed people, "called out" to bring light into darkness.*

The indigenous revolution in the Indian church operates under the radar, is often led by young people, and is guided by the same principles that shaped the early church. While in some ways we are worlds away, I believe that this Christ-ward movement in India has many implications for your churches and your people at this moment in time.

Read *Unleashed* prayerfully, and in a spirit of anticipation for however or wherever the Spirit might lead. I have been praying that more than ever before, we can come together as brothers and sisters to see the name of Jesus proclaimed; *his love and power unleashed from person to person and village to village—both in India and in your communities at home.*

To this end, and in his name,

Sam Stephens,
President of India Gospel League

Chapter 1
Where in the World Is the Church Headed?

The 2016 film *Lion* tells the true story of Saroo Brierley, who at five years old gets lost on a train and ends up nearly a thousand miles from his home in India. Saroo's older brother, Guddu, sometimes does night work, sweeping out train cars to help support his family. One night, after much begging, he reluctantly allows Saroo to join him. Guddu orders Saroo to stay on a bench while he works, and it is there that Saroo falls asleep and wakes to find his brother missing. He boards a train to look for him and, exhausted, falls asleep again, this time aboard a train car. He wakes to find the train moving but is unable to escape. When the train finally stops, he is far from his hometown—the name of which he can't recall at his young age. Saroo wanders the streets of Kolkata for several weeks and is finally taken to a children's home where he is later adopted. It takes twenty-five years for him to find his village and to be reunited with his family.

Saroo was just a child when he innocently boarded the train that night. He was sleepy, disoriented, and alone. He drifted off to sleep and then drifted far, far from his home and family. How terrifyingly simple it was for this little boy to get so very lost. After hearing this story for the first time, it occurred to me that as terrifyingly simple as it was for five-year-old Saroo to get so very lost, the same can be true for us. We just get a little sleepy, become a little disoriented, strike out alone, and, before we know it, we've drifted a thousand miles from where we are supposed to be.

The Drifting Church

Recently as I've traveled, speaking at churches and visiting with friends, I've heard concern that the Western church seems to be suffering from "mission drift." In other words, leaders are seeing incremental movement away from the purposeful mission of going into all the world, making disciples, baptizing them, and teaching them to obey all Jesus taught. Some friends have expressed private concern that perhaps the church in the West will no longer be a significant player in the world. These workers and leaders love the Lord, invest sacrificially, and preach the word in season and out. Yet they, and many other Christian workers, are discouraged by what they observe: flagging interest in missions, a sense that "we've already tried that," and an established consumer church culture. After long seasons of pushing against the tide, some find themselves unsure of how to turn around and find their way "home."

I don't think my friends are alone in their assessments. When I'm in the States, I read the news and Christian journalism. Regardless of the source, the dominant headlines read something like, "Christianity in a Fierce Battle—Appears to Be Losing." Of course, this change has not happened in a vacuum. The battle and associated losses have come from decades of the erosion and redefinition of truth. This has led to a Western culture that is decidedly post-Christian, a culture where numerous threats loom.

Nominal Christianity, which has been the norm in Europe for the past century and a half, has spread across the pond and infiltrated the States. Isolated Christianity, where some have called for believers to "hide out" and shelter in place while the culture burns, is gaining appeal. Youth and millennials are leaving the church in droves. The fastest rising "religious" group is the "Nones" *(or those who identify themselves as having no religious affiliation at all).* And, of course, there are ever more violent swings of the culture wars over every conceivable issue: to kneel in protest or not to kneel; to eat this chicken sandwich or that one; to bake a wedding cake or not; to welcome refugees or build a wall.

Why Me?

At this point, you may be wondering but are too polite to ask, "What is an Indian guy doing weighing in about problems in the Western church?"

It's true—I'm Indian through and through. I'm "of the soil." My family has lived in Tamil Nadu as far back as anyone can recall. But in the mid-nineteenth century, my great-grandfather came to Christ, and God changed the trajectory of my family's destiny and thereby mine as well. For over forty years now, I've been planting and pastoring churches, discipling men and women, and stewarding a piece of the historic work that God is doing in India. Because an East/West partnership is part of India Gospel League's DNA, I've had the privilege of cultivating significant relationships with Western Christian leaders and workers. Those relationships have formed essential pieces of my ministry ethos and practice. At the same time, they have uniquely positioned me to see the strengths and weaknesses of the Western church from an "outside" perspective and then to honestly dialogue with my friends about what I see.

There are several reasons I feel called to have a conversation with the Western church at this specific moment in time. First, I've been asked. Some of the same friends and co-laborers who will weigh in on this book have urged me to pull the curtain back on what God is doing in India today. I've been living and breathing a gospel explosion in India for the past four decades. My American friends have asked me to peek my head out of this work and to consider that at this point in history, when the focus of evangelical growth has shifted to Africa and Asia, the Eastern church has unique thought leadership and insight to offer the West.

Second, an "outside eye" always lends a fresh perspective. Have you noticed how much you "see" when you first enter a new situation like a job, or a church, or even a country? After a bit of time passes, you become acclimated, and it is much more difficult to distinguish obvious needs and assets. "Acclimation blindness" sets in quickly, often within a few weeks! All of us, I'm sure, find outside counsel personally helpful for the very reason that when we invite people into the "world" of our thoughts, they often see with clarity bits and pieces that have faded into the background for us. This is true in our personal lives and in organizations, so why then would it not be valuable from one culture to another in the context of the global church? I have not organized my life around being an outside eye or a consultant to Western churches. However, with the help of my friends (the outside eyes in my life), I have come to see that God has indeed given me a distinct position from which to create a dialogue with Eastern and Western believers.

Finally, I am compelled to testify. Persecution, poverty, and oppression are all around, yet we are witness to a historic movement of the Holy Spirit. Millions of people are coming to Christ, and not primarily through the work of dispatched, seminary-trained pastors but because of friends, family members, and neighbors—new believers—all eager to share what has been incredibly good news for them.

My long-time friend Jim Lyon tells me that he often hears believers describe a longing to go to Israel. Jim says, "When they tell me they want to 'walk where Jesus walked and see the Bible come alive,' I tell them to go to India. Go to India, and the Bible will come alive. Because that's where people still walk in sandals and they still worship idols carved with human hands." Jim describes his many visits to India as "experiencing the Acts of the Apostles." Demons are cast out, lepers are healed, the lame walk, the blind see. We are privileged to see, in real time, spectacular, organic, indigenous church growth—a flash of what it must have been like in the first century days. While the Western church struggles to maneuver under heavy centuries of tradition and institutionalism, India's tiny churches emerging out of a pre-Christian world are stripped down, agile, able, and willing to multiply.

I want to invite you into this incredible moment in time. I am so grateful for the decades of fellowship I've enjoyed with my Western brothers and sisters. We have found great joy in encouraging and sharpening each other through many adventures and late-night conversations. I want to invite you also into this adventure and to join in the conversation. I pray that I can share what God has taught me in a way that is useful to your church at this particular moment in history.

While I am Indian, my work is in India, and God is *certainly* doing something unique in India right now, I believe that what I have to share is widely useful—not only in an Indian context. The principles that I want to dig into are timeless and transcultural. They represent God's will for all Christians.

Join the Adventure

These days, my heart is captivated by a great tension. I see a tremendous open door for the gospel in unreached areas. I see God moving in amazing ways. On the other hand, despite this opportune time (a *kairos* moment, if you will) it seems the traditional church is not geared up to step through the door that God has opened. I think and pray about this often. It's time for multiplication! We can all be part of it! But there are mechanisms in Western church culture, history, and tradition that are slowing the church down. These encumbrances have rendered the church less able to mobilize with flexibility and agility. Let's admit these faults and face them together. Let's look with fresh eyes at how the Lord works. I believe he has much to say that can reorient us to vital, dependent, and fruitful service.

If you are weighed down or discouraged by the slow drift (or rapid crash) of Christianity in the West, I want to encourage you with some unchanging truth. I *know* you know this, but you may need to be reminded. God is not losing, even if what is "seen" indicates otherwise. We know intellectually that he is winning. He *will* have victory. This is, after all, what scripture promises! These promises, however, are not made for intellectual assent alone. We can bank on them, we can live out of them, our expectations can be adjusted to them, and when we do, we can look forward to their fulfillment with hope.

God's word tells us that he is winning in the world. If we are not seeing it, we may just need to know where to look. I want to show you how he is capturing the hearts of a nation in India. And I want to help you see where God is working in your own community. God is doing something big. Don't miss it! Are you ready to join in?

If we want to participate in what God is doing in the world right now, time *is* of the essence. Lingering, waiting, and doing the same old things the same old way will result in missing out on today's window of opportunity. Will the Lord provide more opportunities? Sure. But why miss out on fruitful investment now?

The world and the church are facing unique challenges as we speak. Each of these challenges requires a real-time response from the church. We can't afford to choose tradition over action. There is a world of human need and spiritual darkness. Although our answer to the darkness has never changed, our ways of moving into it must.

We're going to spend the bulk of this book unpacking how we see God working in this unique moment. We'll look at where the growth in the Indian church is coming from; how, specifically, the Spirit is moving; and how we can go along for the ride, planting and harvesting in the fields where God is working. There is much to be learned by taking note of how God is moving in the world. As the Western church moves to work where God is working, not only will it learn from the church in the developing world, but it will see rejuvenation and flourishing in its own backyard.

In order to place the Western church as a whole in this story accurately, let's first take a good, hard look at the challenges and realities you're facing in your churches, cultures, and Christian communities.

REFLECT

1. What do you think about the assessment that the Western church has "drifted" away from its commission to go into the world, making disciples, baptizing, and teaching them? Consider your own fellowship and ministry as well as the Western church as a whole.

2. I have said that "God is winning" in the world. From your vantage point, how do you see this truth unfolding? If you feel you are missing out, how do you imagine you could experience some of this victory?

3. In order to better utilize the material in the coming chapters, take a few prayerful moments and describe how the Lord is uniquely working through your local church body to make a spiritual impact on the community it is serving. How has this work impacted you personally? How has it impacted your church body as a whole?

CHALLENGE

And Jesus came and said to them, "All authority in heaven and on earth has been given to me. Go therefore and make disciples of all nations, baptizing them in the name of the Father and of the Son and of the Holy Spirit, teaching them to observe all that I have commanded you. And behold, I am with you always, to the end of the age." (Matthew 28:18–20 ESV)

1. What does discipleship look like in your church? Describe how it takes place, who is involved, and what you perceive to be the goals.

2. On a scale of 1–10, if one is "very little personal discipleship" and ten is "high involvement in personal discipleship," how would you rate your church on its commitment to discipleship?

   1   2   3   4   5   6   7   8   9   10

3. What does "going to the ends of the earth" look like in your church? Describe how this happens, who is involved, and what you perceive to be the goals.

4. On a scale of 1–10, if one is "very little support of missions" and ten is "high involvement in missions," how would you rate your church on its support and involvement in local and in global missions?

   1   2   3   4   5   6   7   8   9   10

KINGDOM VOICES

Jim Lyon
General Director, Church of God Ministries

Jesus said, "if anyone wants to be my disciple, he must be where I am. For my servants must follow me. And my father in heaven will honor those who honor me" (John 12:26). Right now churches all across the land are wrestling with the questions: How do we disciple? How do we make disciples? What's my next discipleship course? What book can we read? How do we decide?

People are reaching for discipling. Jesus says, "Anyone who wants to be my disciple has to be where I am" (Matthew 16:24). It's the key to everything. Anyone who presumes to follow Jesus must be where Jesus is. Well, where is Jesus? We know that he's ascended to the right hand of the Father. I know that he's in heaven. I know that he's coming back. I know that he's with me. So, in some mysterious way, he's "out there," but he's also here. He's here.

What did he mean when he said you have to be where I am? He was talking in response to some Greeks who came up to find Jesus, to meet Jesus. So this is his reply to them. You want to meet me? You have to go where I am. You can't go where you want to go; you have to go where I am. You can't meet me on your terms. You must meet me on my terms. You intersect with me when you are present, doing the things that I choose to do.

I want to be where Jesus is. Now. And where is he? How do I get those clues? Where is Jesus walking now? How is he animating the body of Christ? We are the body of Christ—the hands of Jesus, the feet of Jesus, the voice of Jesus, the ears and the eyes of Jesus. To be the body of Christ is not just some kind of euphemism. It's a reality between the first and second coming of Christ. We are the physical manifestation of the living Lord. Where is he?

As I think about where Jesus is, I think about India. Of course, Jesus is with me in my place where I live. I've pastored two churches—one in Seattle for twenty years and one near Indianapolis for twenty-two years. I know Jesus is there. And my heart is for those two places. I still pray for those two churches every day.

India is where Jesus is. Of course, he's in Haiti too. Of course, he's in the streets of Santiago. Of course, he's on the streets of Beirut, which are right now in flame. But India's the place where I have gone and met Jesus. And when you kneel down and you help a leper navigate food served on a banana leaf, because the digits of their hands cannot hold a spoon, you cannot escape the reality that Jesus would be here. This is how I'm discipled. This is how I experience life—to be able to come close to people in desperate need. Being with Jesus in India makes me come home and look for people in need in my place. If you want to be a disciple of Jesus, you have to go where Jesus is. That's how you get discipled.

Everyone can't go to India, and you can be discipled without going there. The Lord can disciple us wherever we are. When I've gone to India, though, it has recalibrated what I do. For everyone who wonders, how do I change my world? How do I follow Jesus? Take some cues from what India Gospel League does. You might find yourself at home, transformed.

chapter 2

THE AMERICAN CHURCH, DRIFTING AND DISMISSED

UNLEASHED

Chapter 2
The American Church, Drifting and Dismissed

Do you feel like your church is fighting an uphill battle these days? I don't think it's all in your head. Many Christian leaders and workers are in the thick of the fight, and statistics bear out that the Western church is struggling. Churches close their doors regularly in the States—at a rate of 4,000 per year. In August of 2017, a church that had stood on a Chicago street corner for over fifty years held its final service. Through that very day, the leaders of the church had labored to share the love of Christ in their community and to be faithful stewards of the word. Sadly, the congregation had dwindled to the point that they could no longer afford the mortgage, and the leaders used their last weeks to help parishioners find new church homes in the area.

Feelings Determine Truth

The cultural climate has changed for Christians. Believers walk through a landscape that would have been unfamiliar even twenty-five years ago. Unlike their parents' generation, young Western Christians are surrounded by peers who don't share their faith. What does it look like to be a person of faith today and to talk about Jesus when the very vocabulary of our faith has been diminished and redefined?

This wholesale cultural change is being propelled forward by the new ways in which truth and feelings are defined and valued. Postmodern thought, which many see as the harbinger of "the death of truth," began to bubble around in academia and among artists and philosophers in the mid-twentieth century. It has now so permeated Western culture that phrases such as "my truth" and "if it works for you" are common and unquestioned. Behind these simple expressions is a massive assumption that truth is subjective and cannot be known. It is now considered arrogant and narrow-minded to make certain kinds of truth claims.

Oddly, no one seems to question whether or not it's true that we should gas up our cars before we leave for a trip. We don't question; we just do it! It doesn't matter whether or not we "feel" we have gas or not. We don't question that 2+2 = 4. We don't debate that gravity exists, nor do we try to live outside of its reality. People who jump out of airplanes use parachutes. On the other hand, questions such as whether God is real or who humans are designed to be—and add to that nearly all moral claims—have been relegated to a fully subjective realm. Many consider these questions to be best answered and understood through the lens of feelings and micro-experience. "If I feel it, it must be true" is the modern litmus test for reality. The culture has elevated feelings and subjective experience, while objective truth and even reason are diminished.

A recent Barna Group survey shows that American millennial believers are sure that sharing Jesus is life-changing and important. That's good news! The study goes on to show that these same young people are reluctant to share their faith in a way that calls for a decision. That is not good news. The verse, "If you confess with your mouth that Jesus is Lord and believe in your heart that God raised him from the dead, you will be saved" (Romans 10:9–10 ESV) is, after all, a hefty truth claim that requires some kind of binary, true/not true response. Sadly, Western culture today is overly sensitive to (read: likely to reject) anything that seems to point to an ultimate truth or that requires a decision about that truth. In response, Billy Graham Center Research Institute director Rick Richardson says that the challenge for this generation is to expand conversations from "this is true for me" to include "and this is true for you, too."

The "Nones"

The surging rise of the "Nones," or those who identify themselves as having no religious affiliation, can't be attributed to one single factor such as the redefinition of truth. There are complex influences, including that many people feel the church has failed them in some way. Most individuals in this cohort have come from, and rejected, a religious (and specifically Christian) background. Traditional means of engaging with and reaching them won't do.

This dynamic is not going away any time soon. Ryan P. Burge at Eastern Illinois University reports that in a March 2019 General Social Survey, 23 percent of Americans surveyed answered the question "What is your religion?" with "no religion." At the same time, 22.5 percent answered "evangelical," and 23 percent said "catholic." These statistics seem rather evenly split, but behind these numbers is the fact that fifty years ago, Nones were only a blip on the radar. Since the early '90s, however, Nones have had consistent surges of growth. This demographic has added percentage points every year in the past decade and is now set to outpace growth in both the evangelical and Roman Catholic churches in America.

The rise of Nones since the '90s is not disconnected from the simultaneous free fall decline in attendance and membership at mainline Protestant churches. Burge says, "The biggest story is that 'no religion' is coming from the mainline. Mainliners are jumping ship." In an article he wrote for *Christianity Today*, he notes that "it is statistically inevitable that those of no religious faith will be the largest group in America in the next five years."

To bring this cultural shift out of the realm of data and into your own lives, you can safely presume that those who describe themselves as Nones have already left your churches. They will not come back through the doors easily because they feel they have "been there, done that."

How are you experiencing this change in your ministry? How do you see your church flexing to respond to this emerging demographic? If it all seems a little too difficult to take in, that's because it is! And the growth of the Nones is but one of the many shifting dynamics that the Western church must consider as it seeks to live out and preach the gospel today.

Nominalism and Post-Christian Culture

Nominalism, or simply put, alignment with a belief system in name only, has been a thinly veiled threat to the church for a long time. Because nominal religion is cheap and easy, it has allowed people with a cultural consensus of Christendom to "pass" as true followers of Jesus Christ. The fallout of nominalism is that it has provoked and hastened a complete rejection of Christianity by large swaths of the culture.

Today, the majority of Americans describe themselves as Christians, and even say that their faith is an important aspect of their lives. Are they practicing Christians, though? Barna uses the following algorithm to designate a "practicing Christian": this person must identify as a Christian, express that their faith is very important to them, *and* attend a church service at least once a month. With the addition of that last qualification—minimal participation in the body of Christ—we find that there is no longer a Christian majority in America. In fact, using this algorithm, Barna's research shows that while most Americans say they are Christians, only one in three American adults can be considered to be "practicing" their faith. The statistics are grim, but I posit that the way this plays out in culture is deadly.

For a reference point, I want to quickly take you on an 8,000-mile journey to my home in India. While Europe and North America are considered post-Christian, India is decidedly pre-Christian. In my country, Christians are a clear minority and are under increasing pressure to stay silent about their faith, even to renounce Christ, or face the consequences. Believers experience real persecution—rejected by their communities, run out of town, homes burned, lives lost. I know these men and women. I love them, grieve with them, counsel them, and along with the community of faith, come alongside to comfort, encourage, and help them rebuild. Of course, we pray for this brutal persecution to end. But more than that, we pray for people to suffer well. We pray for them to experience a deep taste of the immeasurable grace of God. We pray that they will learn to rely more and more on his abundant strength and that they will live out of the hope they have in Christ. We pray that they as individuals and the body of Christ will shine like bright lights in their villages. We ask that they stand firm in their faith, are steadfast in love, and are bold in preaching the Good News. We pray that *in the midst* of persecution, the church will thrive.

In my country, claiming the name of Christ comes with a price. As a matter of fact, in 2019, India moved into the "top 10" countries cited for persecuting Christians. It is designated as an "extreme persecution" area. Few here choose to follow Jesus without sincerely counting the cost; nominalism holds very little reward. In contrast, for centuries in Europe and in North America, claiming Christ came with a fair amount of social capital. It meant you were part of the group, in step with the norm, and had access to the "club." Membership in a church might mean networking opportunities for work or rubber-stamp approval when running for the school board. It might lead to political access or power. It might mean that you are automatically seen as a "good" person. It has commonly come to communicate a direct correlation with a particular political party or point of view.

Today in post-Christian Western culture, the descriptor "Christian" is largely nominal. It is often viewed as no more than a box to check among "Buddhist," "Muslim," or "Other." Once the name "Christian" is diluted and divorced from a life-changing relationship with Christ and his church, all sorts of negative fallout begins.

Imagine you are an unbelieving observer in an average American town. Here, almost everyone would check "Christian" on a survey form. Now, take a look around. Only one out of every three people you meet gathers with other believers regularly at a church. Most never read the Bible. Your neighbors define "success" as wealth, education, attractiveness, accumulation, and advancement. When people are successful, you witness sophisticated self-promotion and wide congratulations. When they fail, you see hiding, fear, blame shifting, and despair. Far and wide, you see people consumed with the cares of the world—the lust of the eyes, the lust of the flesh, and the boastful pride of life.

After a few months of observation, what would you understand a "Christian" to be? In times of your own troubles, would you seek out one of these people? Would you be interested in attending a huge church that seems to have a revolving door at the front? At best, you might feel confused about what it means to be a Christian. At worst, you would *not* feel confused but would instead be fairly certain that you knew what it means to be a Christian—to be just like everyone else in your community, but with the added burden of occasionally attending a church where you have no relationships and simply go to sing songs or listen to a teaching that will be forgotten within the hour.

Am I being too harsh? In 1958, John Stott said in his classic book, *Basic Christianity*:

"The great scandal of Christendom today [is] so called 'nominal Christianity.' In countries to which Christian civilization has spread, large numbers of people have covered themselves with a decent, but thin veneer of Christianity. They have allowed themselves to become somewhat involved, enough to be respectable but not enough to be uncomfortable. Their religion is a great, soft cushion. It protects them from the hard unpleasantness of life, while changing its place and shape to suit their convenience. No wonder the cynics speak of hypocrites in the church and dismiss religion as escapism."

Please remember that I regularly work with and count among my closest friends a huge number of pastors and workers in Western churches where their communities cannot be described as nominal. I know that God is bigger than all of the circumstances elsewhere. I know he is still in the business of transforming lives, and I know that he desires to reach those who think they are Christians but who do not know Jesus. We serve the great "I Am," who calls us to himself, rescues us by his grace, and then radically begins to transform us into loving, sacrificial servants. At the same time, the poison embedded within nominal Christianity cannot be overstated. We must take the strongest stance against messages that communicate Christianity as being anything less than a vital, life-changing relationship with the living God.

Stott recognizes the bitter fruits of nominalism: that the church will be discredited, and our faith largely dismissed. It is no wonder that after centuries of unchecked nominalism, Europe is decidedly "post-Christian," and the rest of the Western world is following right behind. The Barna Group recently published sobering statistics that correlate with Stott's observation from 1958. The group has identified a set of factors that include disbelief in God; no participation in prayer, Bible reading, or study; no church attendance; and describing oneself as atheist or agnostic. If a person meets 60 percent or more of these markers, Barna categorizes them as post-Christian. According to this metric, 48 percent of American adults—almost half—are considered as such.

The Flight of Youth and Millennials

If almost half of American adults are post-Christian and over half of adults who claim to be Christians are nominal, it is no wonder that their children are losing interest, and rapidly. Grievously, 58 percent of millennials who grew up in churches have dropped out. David Kinneman, president of Barna Group, points out that "it is . . . sobering to consider the 'de-evangelistic' clout of those who leave the faith." Essentially, individuals who grow up in the church and then leave have testimonies too. They are testimonies of the perceived failure, and perhaps the real failure, of the church. Our enemy, then, finds it easy to tease this perception out to suggest that God himself has failed, or, worse, has failed to exist at all. An entire cultural experience, often called "exvangelical," is growing up around these testimonies.

Millennials are heading out the doors of the Western church rapidly now, but the truth is that for decades, the Western church has struggled to hold onto its youth. Ten years ago, Barna found that a majority of church-going teens left the church after they turned fifteen, either permanently or for an extended period of time. Kinneman, who headed the research, identified six contributing factors, two of which stand out to me: "churches are overprotective" and "the teen experience at church is shallow." Some have said that the Western church preaches a "gospel of niceness" to children. "Niceness" is sorely inadequate to help students meet the real needs in their lives and does not connect with their desires to make significant impacts on the world around them. If Christian parents have niceness and being "good" as their functional goals, then those goals will end up being benchmarks of spirituality rather that a significant Christ-love that impacts others.

The loss of youth is a harbinger of holistic decline. Scott McConnell, executive director of Lifeway Research, says, "The reality is that Protestant churches continue to see the new generation walk away as young adults. Regardless of any external factors, the Protestant church is slowly shrinking from within." This is very bad news, indeed, and we must do all we can to right it.

I am the father of nine children, and I live on a campus that houses three hundred kids at any given time. I'm philosophically passionate about the role of young people in the Kingdom of God. And my heart breaks at these sad truths. I truly believe that the flight of American youth from the church has to do with a self-focused version of Christianity, which of course is not the gospel message at all. Young people are accordingly bored and uninspired by the worldly message of "live your own best life." If we are truly going to engage our young people and keep them in our fellowship, we must become less self-focused and become more gospel focused. We must stop looking inward and start looking outward.

Self and the Strategies of Satan

By concentrating day and night on your feelings, potentials, needs, wants, and desires and by learning to assert them more freely, you do not become a freer, more spontaneous, more creative self; you become a narrower, more self-centered, more isolated one. You do not grow, you shrink.

This observation was made by NYU research sociologist Daniel Yankelovich almost forty years ago. (Apparently millennials and Gen Zers can't be solely blamed for the self-absorption of the Instagram age.) Self. Self-centered, self-absorbed, self-serving, "selfies." Self is a very human thing. And self-absorption is the particular playground of our enemy—the Evil One. After all, it was he who suggested a "self-improvement plan" to Adam and Eve in the garden. It was he who laid out a stunning tapestry of temptations in the desert, each designed to hit chords of self-preservation and self-promotion in the human heart. When Peter suggested that Jesus preserve rather than sacrifice his life at the cross, Jesus stunned him by calling him "Satan."

A friend of mine who helps lead a church in the States recently shared her observation on the American church's adoption of the "self" values of the culture. She rightly noted that our "flesh" is always and automatically moving toward self-service. Satan strategically stokes the fires of self in order to "shrink" our hearts and our impact. My friend believes that the Western church has been diverted from much spiritual victory because of Satan's action on this particular battlefield.

Brothers and sisters, the church must not be blind to this war that has been waged since the garden. Satan went after God's first creation. He went after Jesus. He ensnared the disciples. What would make us think that he is not using the same tried and true strategies on us, right now, in our hearts and in our churches? Is it not possible, is it not likely, that some of the drifting and dismissal of the Western church is directly tied to the self-focus of its members? And how can we not see this as a significant loss in the spiritual battle for the Kingdom?

Where Is Hope?

Love grows cold when self reigns supreme. Moral and ethical scandals are shaking entire denominations and seemingly solid evangelical churches. Culture wars are fought day in and day out on social media. And political parties use Christianity for a marketing scheme. As a result of these and other factors discussed so far, somewhere between one hundred and two hundred churches close their doors each week in the United States.

This chapter has been difficult for me to write. I feel as if I'm standing under the battering ram of statistics, breaking down the sugarcoating spread over the deterioration of the Western church. I know it may have been even more difficult for you to read. These are your people, your sheep, your children.

The particular statistics we've looked at so far tell a story about one place and one time in history. There is, however, another story that *has its genesis before time began and has been repeated over and over again*. Despite what's happening in any particular culture or demographic at a given moment, despite any season of stagnation or decline, despite any ebb and flow in your own work, God is winning, and his Kingdom will be victorious. There is hope. He tells us so.

Hope in Certain Victory

Let's take a moment to meditate on some of these truths found in the word:

- Jesus tells Peter, ". . . I will build my church, and the gates of hell shall not prevail against it" (Matthew 16:18 ESV). The word *prevail* is better translated "withstand." Jesus describes his church as a force to be reckoned with, a power that moves again and again to free those bound by the shackles of our enemy.

- In John's vision recorded in Revelation 7, he describes evidence of God's victory at the end of time, "After this I looked, and behold, a great multitude that no one could number, from every nation, from all tribes and peoples and languages, standing before the throne and before the Lamb, clothed in white robes, with palm branches in their hands, and crying out with a loud voice, 'Salvation belongs to our God who sits on the throne, and to the Lamb!'" (Revelation 7:9–10 ESV). It's simple but true: the existence of the church at the end of time is evidence that God wins!

- In his letter to the Ephesians, Paul declares that Jesus loves the church and gave himself up for her, that he cleansed her and made her holy so that she can one day be presented as his bride—radiant, without stain, wrinkle, or blemish; holy and blameless (Ephesians 5:25–27). The church is the bride of Christ, and he himself is readying her for the marriage feast of the Lamb. That sounds like victory to me!

- Victory doesn't always look the way we expect it should. Frankly, our human vision of a victorious life is often opposed to God's as described in his word. In his vision, John saw Jesus say this to the church in Philadelphia: "I know your works. Behold, I have set before you an open door, which no one is able to shut. I know that you have but little power, and yet you have kept my word and have not denied my name" (Revelation 3:8 ESV). The church didn't have power by any human estimation, but they had a door that God held open. Although victory and power are not correlated, the victorious hand of God—the open door for his work—is apparent in a church that stands on God's word and lives in dependence on him.

- Praise the Lord, the church will stand at the end! The church will be made ready for her Bridegroom, and the church will continue to batter the gates of hell until that day when she is presented to him as his bride. Despite what we may see around us, that victory is unfolding now! Let's not miss it!

Victory in Unexpected Places

What if God's big work in the twenty-first century is *not* primarily in Western cities and suburbs? What if, in fact, the most responsive fields are in the developing world, where believers are now often referred to as Majority World Christians. For a moment, let's move our attention to how and where God's Spirit is working and winning. Let's see where the church is growing. Let's look at the developing world and, specifically, my home—India.

The numbers in the graphic that follows represent the evangelical growth, as ranked by Operation World, in the top forty and the bottom forty countries of the world.

Countries with the fastest growing evangelical population

Countries with the slowest growing (or fastest declining) evangelical population

COUNTRY	ANN GR	COUNTRY	ANN GR
Iran	19.6%	Niue	-4.1%
Afghanistan	16.7%	Sweden	-0.6%
The Gambia	8.9%	Georgia	-0.6%
Cambodia	8.8%	Japan	-0.4%
Greenland	8.4%	Slovenia	-0.2%
Algeria	8.1%	Tokelau Islands	-0.1%
Somalia	8.1%	Falkland Islands	-0.1%
Mongolia	7.9%	Finland	-0.1%
Kuwait	7.3%	United Kingdom	0.0%
Tajikistan	6.9%	Cocos (Keeling) Islands	0.0%
India	3.9%	United States	0.8%

Although all forty countries are not listed here, the forty fastest declining countries include thirteen Western countries, while the forty fastest growing include only two: Greenland and Luxembourg. India is just outside the top forty group for growth, while the United States sits at number thirty in forty countries where evangelical growth is most in decline.

There's a lot to consider here. Factors such as whether a country is pre-Christian or post-Christian matter. As an example, some of the tremendous growth you see here is correlated to the fact that several of these countries are pre-Christian; Afghanistan, for instance, has a population which is only .03 percent evangelical. In comparison, 2.2 percent of Indians identify themselves as evangelical. A study of these complexities is outside the scope of this book, but I'd like us to just sit back and take a look at the obvious trend: the gospel is really taking off in certain places—in fact, in unexpected places. It's worth taking note of where.

Victory in Collaboration

I'd like to suggest that the hope for the Western church, at this moment and perhaps unexpectedly, lies in participating in what God is doing in the *rest of the world.* At this moment in history, there is a great movement of the Spirit among "the least of these" and those who have never heard the gospel. Doesn't it make sense for the Western church to concentrate its efforts where people are responding most to the outpouring of God's Spirit?

Here are three ways I see that a collaboration could greatly benefit the Western church in its time of need.

1. **Obedience** – Wouldn't it be wonderful to know that your church is making significant traction in carrying out the Great Commission? Don't you want your community to be part of that great thread in church history, responsive to Christ's command, "Go"? The most effective way to participate in the Great Commission may look different now than it has ever been imagined, but the call to participate is still being made on the life of every believer. Let's join together in obedience to see his will accomplished here on earth!

2. **Fruit** – There is no doubt that where God's Spirit is working, fruit is born. From my observation, many churches in the United States are filled with believers who love the Lord and are called according to his purposes, but who have long been discouraged by the lack of evangelical fruit. If your local body of Christ is laboring in a difficult field, the fruit of new believers and new spiritual life may be sparse. Perhaps you work with people who seem to be more and more invested in home-improvement projects, straight A's in school, and traveling sports teams. Maybe your congregation has aged and not yet

replicated itself. Yours may be a church of believers who've been saved for decades and whose circles of influence have diminished over the years. If any of these circumstances are true, imagine the effect of directing the hearts and desires of your people to invest across the world in places where "the harvest is plentiful but the workers are few" (Matthew 9:37 NIV). Investing where God is working—no matter where it may be—is the way to begin to see spiritual fruit again!

3. **Excitement** – Of course, to a person whose heart has been transformed by the Lord, obeying the Lord and seeing the resulting fruit is *really* exciting! It's what life is about! And just as inertia and discouragement are contagious, so is excitement! Even more so, the human heart craves eternal significance. You'd be surprised at how quickly I've seen American churches rally with ownership and excitement as they begin to put their hands to the plow of the Great Commission!

Victory Through an Outward Perspective and Significant Work

In Kingdom economy, health and flourishing happen as individuals tend to the health and flourishing of others. And *churches* grow in health and vitality as they look outside of themselves to contribute to the flourishing of others! So how might the Western church grow in health and flourish? In partnership with what's happening in the rest of the world, believers will get to be part of the Great Commission all around the world. They will see fruit and experience a growing sense of significance and excitement. They will witness with their own eyes the kind of organic and contagious Kingdom growth that they may have only read about. They will experience the unique beauty of sitting at the feet of the least of these, to learn from them and "catch" the fire of their joy and confidence in the Lord.

Although the church in the West can't go back to the receptiveness of a pre-Christian field, it can certainly participate in God's victory elsewhere. This experience can happen as it joins in wherever God is working—across the ocean and at home.

In the next chapter, we'll start exploring what it looks like to pay attention to where God is working, to see and seize the moments in which the Spirit is moving in a particular way. We'll also begin to look at the barriers and opportunities that are part of "how" we do ministry. We want to approach these moments with wineskins that allow God's work to shine rather than wineskins which highlight tradition and form. I think you'll find that while I'm largely talking about how God is working in India today, the principles we'll dig into are electric for any church, in any place, at any time.

REFLECT

1. Imagine that someone was able to show you a video that depicted the Western church twenty years from now. What do you think that landscape might look like? Describe your first reaction to that imagined future. Based on the future outcome that you are imagining, would you do anything different from what you are doing now? What would change, and what would stay the same?

2. Are you experiencing "exvangelicalism"? What is your church's approach to reaching the Nones? What would you say is the proportion of nominal Christians in your church, and how do the workers in your church attempt to persuade people away from nominalism?

3. How might your church's teens be "overprotected"? Do you believe they can make a significant impact? How?

4. What do you think about the proposition that hope for the Western church lies in participating in what God is doing in "the least of these" countries?

CHALLENGE

1. Read Luke 14:15–24 (NLT):

    > Hearing this, a man sitting at the table with Jesus exclaimed, "What a blessing it will be to attend a banquet in the Kingdom of God!"

    > Jesus replied with this story: "A man prepared a great feast and sent out many invitations. When the banquet was ready, he sent his servant to tell the guests, 'Come, the banquet is ready.' But they all began making excuses. One said, 'I have just bought a field and must inspect it. Please excuse me.' Another said, 'I have just bought five pairs of oxen, and I want to try them out. Please excuse me.' Another said, 'I just got married, so I can't come.'"

    > "The servant returned and told his master what they had said. His master was furious and said, 'Go quickly into the streets and alleys of the town and invite the poor, the crippled, the blind, and the lame.' After the servant had done this, he reported, 'There is still room for more.' So his master said, 'Go out into the country lanes and behind the hedges and urge anyone you find to come, so that the house will be full. For none of those I first invited will get even the smallest taste of my banquet.'"

    Verse 15 says, "What a blessing it will be to attend a banquet in the Kingdom of God!" We learn from this story that the King's dinner invitation to join in the feast goes out to a broader and broader "audience." If you consider this truth in terms of people groups, or even countries, how might you describe those who joyfully accept the invitation? Now consider the responsiveness of those in the West and the responsiveness of those in India in the context of this story.

What insights do you discover?

2. Timothy 2:15 says, "Do your best to present yourself to God as one approved, a worker who does not need to be ashamed and who correctly handles the word of truth" (NIV). Many millennials say that they are reluctant to share the gospel with their friends. Are we adequately equipping them as approved workers? Knowing the word gives confidence and courage, what are new ways we can challenge and equip millennials with the spiritual weapons they need?

KINGDOM VOICES

Reggie McNeal
Missional Leadership Specialist, Leadership Network

There is a massive disconnect between what's going on in the church as an institution and the church as a movement. The church as movement is gathering steam. In fact, it's rocking and rolling. And the church as an institution, for the most part, is unaware of that or is ignoring it. The difference is that church as an institution is just church-centric, whereas church as a movement is Kingdom-centric.

Some people look at the church through Kingdom lenses, but others look at the Kingdom through church lenses. And those lenses are different. This is why most church renewal efforts are doomed to fail. And every denomination I know of is in some kind of church reclamation effort, reinvigorating, or whatever.

The point is, when the church is not on the right mission, you can pour all of the money and effort and stuff into putting paddles on the corpse, and you can get it to jump around a little bit, but if that sucker is not alive with what the mission is, it doesn't matter. People who are locked into church as institution just can't figure it out. They think, *Let's double down on what is not working.* And that keeps them busy. And busyness is often a form of denial, right? We can take busyness in lieu of vitality and vibrancy.

So much of our discipleship efforts are not about creating disciples of Jesus. We're creating disciples of the church. In crass terms, it's called "customer service." And we're creating customers. And then we have to feed the customer base with programming. Because you can run a program church off of whoever will pay the ticket. It just takes time and money. You keep bringing people in—who you can suck the life out of—to keep the church going.

Or, you can actually connect people with Jesus and the Kingdom and watch them *be* the church. You'll be amazed at the energy and the power and the life and the impact. That's what you yearn to see. That's what the Western church wants to see. But until it confesses its idolatrous position—not just being missionally misaligned but actually running a counter mission—we're just competing against the Kingdom of God and what God wants to do.

Jim Lyon
General Director, Church of God Ministries

We can see a dividing line in the words "in the world but not of the world." But we don't even go in the world. And that creates huge gaps of understanding with the world. To be "indigenous," I have to actually be in the world. I have to be in that community. I have to be in that place. And that is sometimes the missing piece in what I call "Western Christianity."

I work with many pastors to try to get them out of what I call "the Christian book ghetto." What I mean by this is that so many of our leaders only read content that is generated by their own community. That's not being indigenous.

When I first went to India in 1987, I was completely overwhelmed. India can be overwhelming. Sam Stephens recommended a book to me called *Freedom at Midnight* by Larry Collins and Dominique Lapierre. I bought that book in an airport in Bombay and then read the whole thing on my way home on the plane. I just devoured it, because it put me "into" India. It's a secular book, and it has nothing to do with Jesus. But that book opened my eyes on what I'd seen on that journey. Now I read all kinds of books about India that have nothing to do with the gospel.

But similarly, in our own country, people have very little traction with anything that's not published with a Christian imprint. They should be reading books that are on the bestseller list. They need to just be more culturally in tune.

Now, I think the new generations, the millennial generation and the one behind, the ones coming up in church leadership in our tribe, are way more culturally competent than the ones before them. And that's because technology has forced it on us. In a smartphone world, you cannot escape diving into the culture differently.

chapter 3

WIND, WINE, AND *KAIROS* MOMENTS

Chapter 3
Wind, Wine, and *Kairos* Moments

If you travel to my home state of Tamil Nadu and drive along the southern coast, you'll see the enormous white wind turbines of the Muppandal Wind Farm towering over palm trees, electric lines, and buildings as far as the eye can see. The wind farm's only barriers are the mountains rising up and around them. Where the mountains are low enough, you'll find the turbines planted right on top of them. As the largest operational onshore wind farm in India, Muppandal's presence, in many ways, illustrates the great push-pull India has experienced over the last few decades. On one hand, cutting-edge technology and wealth creation are full steam ahead. On the other, underdevelopment and poverty are still undeniably present.

In the midst of this interesting dichotomy, India is competing and excelling globally in the area of renewable energy, specifically wind energy. Today India has the third and fourth largest onshore wind farms in the entire world! These farms have the capacity to supply 10 percent of the energy share in India today. (For comparison's sake, wind powers just over 6 percent of the energy base in the US.) All of this is exciting. All of this is good. I'm glad for wind power. There is, however, one caveat. Sometimes the wind doesn't blow. Entire areas can experience what's called "wind drought." Who knew?

If you've ever seen the double- or triple-long eighteen-wheelers required to transport even one blade of a wind turbine, you know how threateningly huge these machines are. Building a wind farm is no small task, and it's not a decision to be lightly considered or implemented. How unfortunate, then, when so much time, money, and energy is invested and the wind dies down or blows elsewhere. Now, as far as I know, wind droughts are not permanent. Eventually, after a few months, weather patterns return to normal and the wind picks up again.

Of course, this book is not about renewable energy, nor is it about wind farms. But it is very much an examination of what it looks like to position ourselves and our ministries in the places where the wind of God's Spirit is blowing—and to work in conjunction with and dependence on what he is already doing. As believers, we need to one-up the wind farms. Yes, let's throw all of our resources to where the wind is blowing now, to where God is working, and then let's be flexible, ready, and able to move when the Spirit moves elsewhere.

Work Where the Wind Is Blowing

Jesus himself is our example of this kind of flexible, dependent life and ministry. As a matter of fact, Jesus Christ, God in the flesh, resurrector and resurrected, said over and over that he would only work where God was working. He would only come alongside. His dependent posture was linked to great power because he was fully, deeply dependent on his initiating, omnipotent Father.

Jesus explained this dependence to his disciples: "Truly, truly, I say to you, the Son can do nothing of his own accord, but only what he sees the Father doing" (John 5:19 ESV). The Son of God operated with eyes wide open. He was on the lookout for and trained to recognize his Father's hand. When he saw it, he joined in. Not before he saw it, not after, but in that moment. At the opportune time. Where and when the wind was blowing.

It's almost mind-boggling to think of the spiritual power, direction, and efficacy to which we have access. In his sovereign wisdom, God initiates, and then God invites, and all we have to do is join in. It seems so simple. (And it is!) Yet in the history of humanity and of Kingdom work, we've built far too many massive, expensive, labor-intensive wind farms in areas where the wind is not blowing.

Automatic Pilot

Let's take a look at this difficulty through another lens. We all know what it's like to be on automatic pilot in our everyday lives. Without even thinking, our nature is to do what we know—to follow well-worn paths. We drive home listening to music and planning for tomorrow's meeting. Do we notice the traffic lights, or the left turns, or even how we got home? Probably not.

Automatic pilot is a subconscious mechanism, but more often than not, even when we're purposefully plotting a course, we choose familiar "roads." The reality is that we get busy, we want to be efficient, and it seems expedient to do the same things in the same ways we've always done them. Of course, there is nothing inherently wrong with doing the same things the same ways. The trouble comes when we're driving home, plotting out our grocery list or replaying a conversation from our day, and we fail to notice a detour sign meant to prevent us from hitting a huge tree that has fallen in the road.

Even more to the point, autopiloting through life can blind us to all kinds of important information that can only be gleaned by close observation of our environment. What is new? What has changed? What is down that side street that we've never explored? What might be happening there next year? Looking up, looking around, asking questions, and most importantly for believers, asking the Lord to be our guide is crucial if we want to be strategic in an ever-changing landscape.

Let's think back on the last chapter, where we covered a lot of "bad news" and asked how in the world we got to the place we are today. I'd like to suggest that one of the answers to "how did we get here?" has to do with having a model of church that values structures, permanence, and well-worn form over Spirit-led direction. Like wind farms built in places where the wind stopped blowing years ago, too many people are stuck in what was built in the past, hoping that the wind will blow there again without looking to see just where God's Spirit is actually blowing now.

Here's an example. In 1980, the well-regarded *Jesus* film had been translated into Hindi and made a first international showing to an estimated 21 million Indian people. Thousands upon thousands upon thousands of people who had no previous idea of who Jesus was, who had never heard of the one true God who lived among us and died to save us, heard the message and gave their lives to Christ. What an amazing provision at that moment in time! How mightily the

Lord worked and used technology, creativity, and access to proclaim his gospel! Now imagine that because the *Jesus* film was so effective in 1980, we decided to invest all of our money in projectors, screens, and theaters and continued to show the film, week after week, on the same city blocks, in perpetuity. Would this decision be wise? Maybe so. If the film was so successful, why not?

Now please don't get me wrong. The gospel is timeless. The gospel bears repeating, week after week, in perpetuity. We believers must preach the gospel to ourselves every day because it is a living message which has daily power to correct and refresh and empower. If we weaken, or God forbid, forget the gospel, we have nothing to live on and nothing to offer.

Not timeless are the means by which we preach the gospel—the forms that carry it out to the ears and hearts of the lost. In fact, as powerful as it once was, the *Jesus* film is no longer an effective tool for evangelism in India. In a climate primed for persecution, large and open rallies, megachurches in huge buildings, and mass conversion efforts are having diminishing returns. Not to mention that as exciting as they are, these huge events do not typically correlate to effective follow-up with new believers or the responsibility of the Great Commission: making disciples. We get into trouble when we expect God to move in the same ways we've seen him move before and expect "spiritual action" in the ways and means it has "always" unfolded.

When we don't see how and where God is actually working, we will ultimately devote our time, money, and spiritual energy to the wrong places. We'll use old wineskins, plant in hard soil, and build windmills where there is no wind. We will use up our energy in human methods rather than relying on living, renewable spiritual power. Most concerning, we will end up training and discipling in methods and "best practices" rather than in godliness and a spirit-led, dependent life.

A *Kairos* Moment

Over the past years, I've thought and shared quite a bit about something I call "*kairos* moments." *Kairos* is an ancient Greek word that describes an "opportune time." For our purposes, this is a moment when everything is ready, when the foundations have been laid, when decisive action must be taken, and when God's prevailing purpose becomes clear. *Kairos* moments are supernaturally initiated. They do not emerge from human wisdom, plans, or effort. Our only job is to notice and respond, to set our sails to meet the wind of the Spirit.

A moment such as this is being realized all over South Asia right now. It is a historic, Spirit-led, Spirit-powered movement. Despite many obstacles to evangelism and the proclamation of the gospel in recent years, men and women, young and old, are responding to Jesus and embracing the Christian faith. God initiated this work. He laid the foundations. He then led India Gospel League (IGL) along so that we could join him in his work. As a result, in the past twenty years, almost 100,000 churches have been planted in villages where the name of Christ was previously unknown. The Kingdom is growing! This is astounding! Praise the Lord!

Of course, numbers can never tell the whole story, as every number represents one unique and precious soul, one person whom God knows and loves deeply. Numbers can, however, capture the scale and scope of what happens when God decides that it is time. I'd like to briefly walk you through an overview of what we are seeing on the ground here in my home country.

In 2018:

- 135,072 individuals were baptized
- 6,899 churches were planted, an average of almost 19 new churches a day
- 6,992 pastors were trained
- 2,755 women leaders were trained
- 965,000 children were discipled through Children's Gospel Clubs
- 6,127 young people were trained to lead Children's Gospel Clubs

Isn't this amazing? Isn't this a clear work of the Lord? These would be remarkable stats for American churches. But for rural Indian churches, you might say these stats are impossible. They are not. We are witnessing a miracle. IGL is positioned to reach the lowest of the low in our world. The poor, women, children, people with special needs, the sick—these people aren't considered to have much worth in India. But God values them, and he is allowing us to reach and care for them by the thousands.

Often when I'm traveling and get introduced to someone, the person doing the introducing will say, "Sam Stephens has planted *x* number of churches," or "IGL has planted *x* number of churches." And I understand what they want to communicate. But let's be clear: it is *God* who is planting the churches. This is not something I say to make an attempt at humility or to appear demure. This is more than a Christian phrase or cliché to me. Jesus said, "I will build my church, and the gates of hell shall not prevail against it" (Matthew 16:18 ESV). We must recognize the fact that God is doing his work, and he is merely including us in it. We must not only recognize that fact, but we must live from it and make it our basis, our foundation, our hope. When we live out from the truth that God is building his church and the gates of hell will not prevail against it, then we see that our work, our effort, and our results are clearly nothing but a privilege to participate, given to us by a generous God.

I am so grateful for that privilege. God is doing his work, and God is doing it in amazing ways. We are going through an incredible time in history when the church is growing in a way that it has never ever grown before. And it's not because of our strategies, not because of our methods, not because of our planning, not because of the resources that are pouring in. This is God's time! And he is moving! It is a *kairos* moment of opportunity. If we as leaders are able to see how it is happening and seize this opportunity to be part of it—this *kairos* moment—then God will multiply his church.

The exponential growth we see today is not a result of traditional missionary methods nor of standard church planting and growth strategies. The growth pattern we're observing is closer to what we read about in the book of Acts and have heard of in the first-century church.

New Wineskins

Each of us is poised for *kairos* moments when our eyes are open to what God is doing and when we are not locked in to "the way it's always been done"—the old wineskins. Jesus said, *". . . no one pours new wine into old wineskins. Otherwise, the wine will burst the skins, and both the wine and the wineskins will be ruined. No, they pour new wine into new wineskins" (Mark 2:22 NIV)*. The liveliness, the energy, the force of all spiritual life is in Jesus Christ himself, our risen savior. He is the wine, bubbling, alive, and life changing.

If anyone ever presents you with a wineskin, it should be obvious where the value lies—in the wine! A wineskin is useful, but it's just the vessel. Its purpose is to hold, transport, and pour the wine, but it's not the main event. The wine is.

I used the *Jesus* film as a "wineskin" example earlier. Let me suggest another example that might pertain to something you are encountering in your communities. Many Christian workers and leaders are noting that because of changes in culture, certain ways of presenting (the wineskin) the Good News (the wine) are less effective than they used to be. By the middle of the last century, great evangelistic campaigns like those of Billy Graham were reaching tens of thousands with a simple message of sin and forgiveness. Of course, sin and forgiveness are central tenets of the gospel message. That hasn't changed. What has changed, however, is that Western culture now has very little sense of what "sin" is. (Thank you, moral relativism.)

Along with a diminished understanding of sin, there is a diminished sense of corresponding guilt. The collective conscience of the culture does not "feel bad" about couples living together before marriage, about gaming the system if the system is deemed to be broken in some way, or about wholeheartedly pursuing material wealth and personal comfort. The culture does not know what sin is, and people don't feel guilty about breaking God's moral law. Why would anyone ever seek a solution to a problem he doesn't think he has?

Because cultural language has moved away from clear definitions of sin and guilt, an old wineskin that uses these words no longer works to effectively communicate the gospel—or to share the wine. Western people may not think that they "sin," but they do recognize that their lives aren't working well. This recognition is an access point for the gospel. We just have to use some different words to get in the door—a new wineskin, if you will.

We are, of course, called to serve in season and out; difficult fields or slow responses are not an immediate cue to pull up camp and move on. To say it another way, a wise worker doesn't grab a new wineskin for each day of the week. A prolonged season of stagnation is, however, a time to prayerfully evaluate our hearts, our ministry ethos, our surrounding field, and the effectiveness of the wineskin we've been using. The truth is that if we've placed our hope in an old wineskin rather than in the moving Spirit of God, we won't see power, and we won't see fruit.

If I were to say just one thing about how to notice a *kairos* moment, or to avoid stagnating in an old wineskin, it would be this: *look to see where God is working, and work alongside him.* Work where God is working. Look to see who is responding to the gospel. Is it someone you didn't expect? Or who doesn't seem to be a "prime candidate" for discipleship? Follow God's lead. Invest. Look to see how God seems to be working in your community. Is it through Sunday services at your church building between 11:00 a.m. and 12:00 p.m.? If not, ask the Lord if it's time to break out of the walls. A fresh perspective comes when we look to see where and how God is working.

I believe there is much that the Western church can learn from our "least of these" churches in India. For the pastors, leaders, and mission-minded Christians who read this book, I'd like to invite you into the *kairos* moment unfolding in India today. I want you to see the story of how God is working in and growing his church here. Again, this is my homeland, my soil, and my area of expertise. The principles God has taught me in my years of ministry here, however, translate to any culture, any community, and any church. I've received so much help and wisdom over the years through personal and collaborative partnerships with friends and churches in the West, and I'm eager to share with you as well.

The story in the next chapter begins with a bit of missions history. We'll take a look at how the gospel first came to India, how it was spread by European missionaries, and how the Indian church, unfortunately, came to mimic Western forms and practices. Next,

I'll describe the exciting Kingdom expansion we are seeing as well as document what I believe is behind it. I want to demonstrate that there is a practical pathway for reaching the unreached, and that there's an established track record of leaving behind a viable, self-sustaining witness. We'll celebrate what God has accomplished so far—many of you have been part of this work—and I'll bring you up to date and we'll savor the harvest together. Finally, I want to show you where I believe God is leading us. Friends, I believe that there is a possibility in the very near future that the Lord will allow us to reach all of unreached India! I want to invite you into that story, and I trust the Lord that he will weave your story into ours in a beautiful way.

REFLECT

1. When was the last time you "changed direction" in order to follow where the Lord was leading? Describe what you thought and felt at that crossroads. What propelled you forward? How did it work out?

2. Sometimes we don't notice the people who are responding to the gospel or to discipleship with zeal because they are not what we consider "prime candidates." Is it possible that you might be overlooking someone like this? Jot down a list of indicators that someone is responsive to the gospel, and then add to that list the names of those in your sphere of influence who seem to match up. Are you surprised by anyone who is on the list? By anyone who is not? What would it look like to "work where God is working" among these people?

3. Which wineskins in your church need to be re-evaluated as to their effectiveness? Have any demonstrated a prolonged season of stagnation? What might work better? If it's difficult to let go of a wineskin that is no longer fruitful, can you describe why? What would it look like to trust God with change in this area?

4. Where do you see the Spirit of God moving in your fellowship or ministry?

CHALLENGE

1. Read these words.

   *"Be very careful, then, how you live—not as unwise but as wise, making the most **of every opportunity**, because the days are evil. Therefore do not be foolish, but understand what the Lord's will is" (Ephesians 5:15–17 NIV).*

   God has called us to respond to *kairos* moments and to redeem the time for his Kingdom. Doing so may challenge your current way of doing ministry. Think back on the last time you saw a genuine *kairos* moment, where you saw yourself or others respond to the gospel in a supernatural way. Has it been a while since you have seen the Holy Spirit move in a way that defies human power? If so, ask God to develop in your heart a Kingdom mentality and show you where he is working. And ask him for an opportunity to participate in that movement.

2. It's human tendency to want to create our own *kairos* moment to stay within our comfort zone, but some of the greatest kairos moments recorded in the Bible called people to step into uncharted territory (Moses and the burning bush, Jesus reaching the Samaritan village through the woman at the well, etc.). Considering your ministry, how much of it has been comfortable? Where have you taken risks for the gospel because you felt the Lord was leading you in that direction? Prayerfully consider what God might be doing outside your paradigm, your church, your family, and your methodology.

3. Maybe you are currently in a situation where you see a great spiritual breakthrough happening close to you, but you are hesitant to join in on that *kairos* moment. Why might that be? What barriers or excuses might you be throwing up in order to stay "safe"?

KINGDOM VOICES

Warren Bird
Researcher and Writer, Leadership Network

Culture is always changing. And when a movement begins, it's the message that connects with people. For example, today we use the word *brokenness*. Ten years ago, we used *felt needs*. And ten years before that, we would have used other words to connect with people. There's always some word or thing that really resonates with a culture at a given time. We can't keep using the equivalent of bus ministry, which worked forty years ago, because now people would say, "I'm not going to trust you today to just take my kids off to church on a bus." Well, God mightily used bus ministry at that time, didn't he? But that was the method, not the message. And sometimes we blur method and message together. We don't know how to separate the method from the message—the truly timeless message.

Let's go back to the word *brokenness* again. If you look in a concordance, *brokenness* isn't there, but you and I would say, "Well, that's what we mean by sin and estrangement from God." *Brokenness* works with today's culture, but ten years from now, *brokenness* most likely won't work. We'd need another term. And that's okay. The message would still be the same. The gospel still fundamentally doesn't change. Jesus doesn't change. So, if what we're doing right now really works, given all that's going on in our culture and the political environment will it still work in ten years? Do we still deliver it the same way? How do we discern? How do we keep tweaking the methodology to fit the current culture?

chapter 4

LOOK BACK TO GO FORWARD

UNLEASHED

Chapter 4
Look Back to Go Forward

An American missionary was traveling to a remote area to preach the gospel and was lucky enough to have a friendly cab driver pick him up at the airport. Soon enough, Christianity came up in their conversation. When the missionary asked the man if he was a Christian, the cabbie said that no, he was not, but he knew what one was, and he could tell if a person was or wasn't a Christian. Intrigued, the missionary asked how, in fact, he could tell whether a person was a Christian.

You are probably hoping his response was, "By their love for one another!" But no. That was not his answer. The cab driver confided that he could tell whether a person was a Christian because he would be wearing pants, as would the men in his group—or his "Church of Pants."

The cab driver dropped the missionary off at his location and drove away. But this idea stuck in the missionary's mind. Later, he learned that Christians who had been there in the past were uncomfortable wearing the traditional robes that the men in that area wore. The Western Christians felt the robes looked like dresses and were feminine. Not only did those Western missionaries insist on wearing pants, but they "discipled" their converts to the religion of pants. They communicated that wearing pants was proper and better for men. The unspoken conclusion became that somehow wearing pants was morally superior to wearing robes, and that good Christian men would be pants wearers—"They will know we are Christians by our pants."

This story is both funny and sad. The practice of missions and our understanding of how to reach a lost world have evolved since then, overcoming significant obstacles, one of those being the practice of conflating culture with godliness, as this story describes. While many positive changes have happened in mission practice, it is important that we are mindful of some of the problems that have been woven into and remain part of the historic missional ethos. To do this, I'd like to step back and trace the history of Christianity in India. After all, it is wise to look back as we move forward. We'll start in the very first days when India was an early church satellite and then move through the First Wave and Second Wave of church growth in the modern period. Over millennia, the trajectory paints a picture of God's work throughout history and his patient pursuit of people in order to make them his own.

India's First Church Plant –
A Wave of Growth from the First-Century Church

Early church history shows that St. Thomas (yes, *that* Thomas) landed in Cranganore, located in the southwest coastal region of Malabar (see the map that follows), in about 52 AD. It is said that he won his first converts from among Jewish traders who had settled there. Other evidence corroborates this tradition: By 345 AD, the church had sent a bishop to India from Jerusalem. And in 530 AD, a traveler journeying through southwest India and Ceylon reported finding Christian communities.

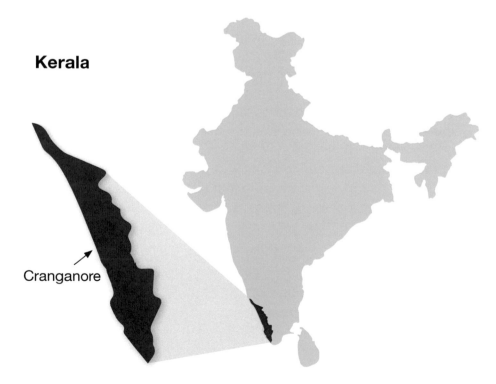

Kerala

Cranganore

Interestingly, this early church plant grew in a way that was distinct from the culture in Malabar and even from the ecclesiastical traditions established in the Greco-Roman world. The Indian Catholic priest and scholar P.J. Podipara described it as "Indian in culture, Christian in religion, and Oriental in worship." In many ways, the church adapted to the local attitude of the southwest Indian coast. Portuguese missionaries arriving in the sixteenth century were surprised to see the extent to which the "Thomas Christians" had adopted the cultural traits and patterns of the surrounding area.

The Thomas Christian community is an interesting proof that Christianity is not only a Western culture religion but also, in fact, Indian Christianity is as old as Christianity itself. This ancient community of Malabar, rooted in the Indian soil, was an indigenous church and stands as evidence of the staying power of the indigenous church over the centuries. Portuguese author Antonio de Gouvea and other writers described the way of life of these Christians. From their descriptions, there is no evidence that these Christians and the faith they practiced seemed "foreign" in any unnecessary way. The people of the Malabar region genuinely accepted these Christians as a part of their society. To some degree, that society also shaped the Christians' understanding and practice of their faith.

This community predated colonialism by centuries, and along with existing outside of Western Christianity, it avoided being enmeshed with the imperial power dynamics that existed later in India. It remains a unique lens into Christian life that is not directly connected to the West. Today in Cranganore, which is located in the modern state of Kerala, Christians are the third most populous religious community. Although they are a minority, they are a disproportionately large group compared to the rest of India.

The First Wave of Growth in the Modern Period

THE FIRST WAVE
- Foreign mission efforts introduce people to the gospel
- Some respond, and the seeds of a movement are planted
- Cultural values are often imported at the gospel's expense

- Missionaries and denominations maintain control of leadership
- Indigenous growth is minimal

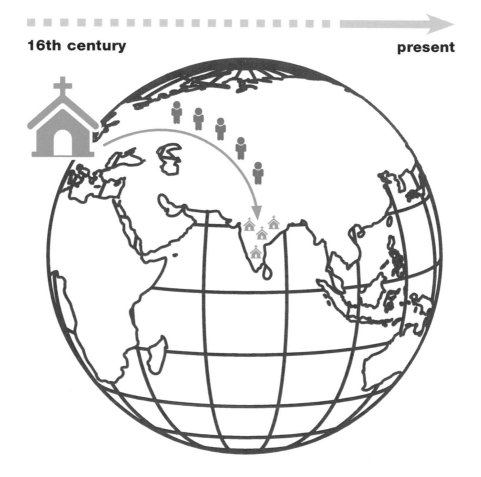

16th century   **present**

The First Wave of church growth in India began with foreign missions in the era of exploration and colonization when the gospel was being taken to the far ends of the earth. Christianity came to India with an emphasis on the Bible, but missionaries embedded it in Western Christian heritage, with little or no room for cultural interpretation. The Good News was clothed in Western garb, and conversion to Christianity meant conversion to Western culture.

We've already talked about how traditional Indian clothing was challenged by Western missionaries. But the issue of music was an even greater and more ubiquitous tension. Without exception, missionaries brought Western tunes, European hymns, and Western instruments wherever they went. (No surprise, organs are not indigenous Indian instruments.) Yes, hymns were translated into local languages, but everything else was foreign to the Indian people. They could not identify with these pieces of imposed culture.

Early missionaries went beyond just importing musical instruments into Indian culture. They actually taught that the use of indigenous instruments was a sin. They also preached that traditional hairstyles were considered "sin" and converts had to do away with them. Likewise, traditional clothing, the dhoti and long robes, were considered "sin." People weren't allowed to attend church in those clothes. To come to church and to be a Christian, they had to dress differently, sing differently, and worship differently than anything they had been used to. Unsurprisingly, none of these surface-level impositions took root in the culture. Disastrously, neither did the transcendent message of the gospel. "Western Christianity" and the gospel along with it, was for the most part, rejected.

Threads of this ministry model (gospel + Western culture) still stretch into India today. People often ask me my perspective on the most pressing threats and dangers faced by the Indian church. It surprises some that persecution and militancy against Christians do not top my list. Rather, one of my greatest concerns is that, even today, the indigenous church in India could become culturally irrelevant as it mimics Western models and methods of "doing church."

In First Wave style ministry, missionaries emphasize shaping new believers around cultural norms. When the target audience is tribal or considered primitive, these norms are introduced along with a healthy dose of condescension. In my experience, both as a barefoot pastor and now as the president of India Gospel League, I can honestly say that the flaws of First Wave style missions diminish any results: I've observed "converts" who do not understand their faith at all. When irrelevant Western culture practices are superimposed and given equal (or greater) standing with scripture, believers lack biblical understanding. When *cultural* transformation is emphasized instead of *spiritual* transformation, the cultural converts are more likely to experience rejection and persecution at home. And, sadly, this happens for reasons that have nothing to do with the gospel of Christ.

It is interesting and important to note that even in a model steeped in condescension, coercion, and cultural supremacy, God's Spirit still speaks through the word of God. Despite human ignorance and failings, he uses efforts made in faith to prepare the soil for the coming harvest. We can give credit to the foreign missionaries who made enormous contributions in language development and in attempts to "translate" Christian concepts, doctrines, and the gospel to the vernacular. Even though flawed, this work paved the way for greater work to come.

Let's take a look at some specific examples of First Wave impact — the good and the bad.

Visit to a Tribal Region

A few years ago, I made a ten-day visit to a tribal area in Jharkhand state called Chota Nagpur, where I planned to serve, teach, and do some field research. I wanted to understand the sociocultural practices of the tribe I visited and why they had become so receptive to the gospel message. A significant number of people in this tribe were embracing the Christian faith. It seemed that they were part of a "Christward movement," which signifies that Jesus Christ and his teachings had attracted them (as opposed to so-called "conversions" primarily motivated by social, political, and economic benefits rather than by the opportunity to have peace with God through Christ).

I found the richness of the Chota Nagpur tribal culture beautiful and was astonished by the similarity of some of their stories and beliefs to core Judeo-Christian stories and beliefs. It seemed that God had paved the way for *his* story! This community believed in one supreme God, while their neighbors worshipped a pantheon of gods and goddesses. The god they worshipped, Darmes, was a creator and sustainer; he was unseen but could be experienced. They told me a favorite story in which Darmes hid a single man and a single woman in his bosom, saving them from a worldwide flood!

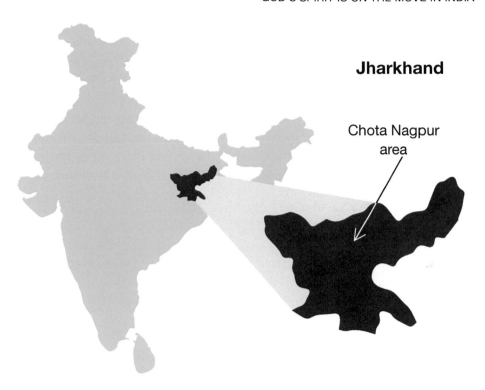

Jharkhand

Chota Nagpur
area

If their stories and beliefs paved the way for news of the one true God, the structure of the tribe paved the way for gospel community. As with many tribal groups, their relational ties are strong, and people are close knit. They don't need to be taught that connection and community are important; it is a value they already share with early church believers.

One hundred and fifty years before my visit, missionaries reached this region. First Lutheran missionaries came, then Anglican, and then Roman Catholics came, all with the goal of evangelizing these tribal people. Since that time, these missionary groups have continued to work independently of one another, and each has seen varying degrees of responsiveness to the gospel. Records of their work reveal that historically the missionaries had a double agenda. They purposed to present the message of Jesus Christ, while at the same time, they each intended to establish their own sectarian governance and faith practices. Not one of them seemed to notice God's revelation of himself within the culture, and missionaries shunned all the indigenous cultural elements, including those that were positive, as "evil" and "uncivilized."

There is almost always a two-tier exclusivity in First Wave style missions—one that continues to this day in many parts of the world. First, there is the proper exclusivity of the message of Christ and his gospel. Second, and to the detriment of the first, are exclusive claims about wineskins—the forms and practical expressions of that message. This second type of exclusivity does not recognize God at work in every culture and among every people.

It is no great surprise that all those years ago, many in Chota Nagpur ignored the gospel message, cloaked as it was with cultural imposition and denominational rigidity. It is also no surprise that today, absent those things, the response to Christ is vibrant and extensive.

The Weight of Colonialism

Do you remember that America was accidentally "discovered" by Christopher Columbus in 1492 on a trip intended to explore and claim a share in the riches of India? Just years after Columbus' misadventure, the Portuguese began to lay claim to India. The French and Dutch soon joined in the jostle for power. Finally, and most pervasively, the United Kingdom began to take control. By the middle of the nineteenth century, England controlled almost all of India.

The Western colonists were universally considered Christians, although they rarely demonstrated interest in Christ. This nominal dynamic played out even as Western missionaries were doing work in India in increasing numbers. Indian converts entered a faith that had been deeply polluted by the nominalism of colonial "Christians." This left believing communities with questions amounting to an identity crisis. Who were they in contrast to colonial Christians from the West? If "Western" and "Christian" belonged together, were they some kind of an inferior subset in the community of faith?

Broad westernization of the gospel complicated even the *way to* Christ. This is tragic because the way to Christ is simple. But colonial Christianity and the missionary Christianity of its time carried heavy burdens. First, Indians saw Christianity as an alien religion. They perceived it this way because colonial missionaries presented it this way. Second, Indians saw Christianity as the religion of colonizers. As a result, when Indian converts shared their newfound faith, they also had to convince others that Christianity did not inherently include oppressive Western colonial power dynamics. Even today, seventy-plus years after Indian independence, the long fingers of colonialism affect how Indian people perceive Christianity. Not only in India, but in many parts of the non-Western world, there is a lingering idea that Christianity is part of a Western identity.

My desire is to preach Christ as a savior who supersedes, embraces, and corrects *all* cultures. The gospel is not Western nor is it Eastern, but it is transcultural. Think about it: the gospel had to be contextualized for Europe and America too. It is not inherently Western! God pursued people and communities in Europe and America by bringing a contextualized gospel to these cultures from its birthplace in Israel. He spoke in a language that allowed them to receive the heart message of Christ and his great sacrifice for them. If only early missionaries would have understood that it wasn't their Western culture that brought salvation but the God who created culture and exists outside of it.

Pushback

In the wake of India's independence in 1947, there has been a long-simmering pushback against Western identity, Western power, and wrapped up in it, Western religion. Surges of celebratory and passionate nationalism have evolved into a new hyper-nationalism and religious fundamentalism: Hindutva, or the Hinduisation of India.

As a result of the rise of Hindutva, missions methods associated with the First Wave of modern church growth have been scrutinized and largely put aside. However, it would be a mistake to assume that all such Western culture packaged, control-heavy work, has ceased. Over time, much of it has evolved into what I describe as the "Second Wave" of missions in India, and it has contributed to a Second Wave of spiritual growth.

As we look at the Second Wave, we'll see once again that, no matter the flaws and mixed motives, where there are efforts made in faith and where God's word is preached, a foundation for greater work is laid.

The Second Wave of Growth in the Modern Period

THE SECOND WAVE

- Foreign mission workers train local leaders
- Strategy shifts toward empowering and equipping
- First Wave workers continue to be involved with leadership, strategy, and resources, Western denominations stay at the helm
- Churches begin to thrive

19th century   **present**

By the end of the nineteenth century, surging nationalism and a bold desire to be free from colonizers had spilled over into the church. Within the local church, people were excited to express their Christian faith in ways that connected with their hearts. The Indian church began to experience an exciting growth spurt! Most of this growth was happening within existing denominational lines and power structures established by foreign missionaries. These communities evolved into what we now commonly recognize as "mainline" churches in India. They are Indian churches, led by Indians, but they are under the umbrella of denominations that embody Western cultural frameworks, theologies, and ways of "doing church."

The Second Wave has been far more effective than the first, both in communicating the gospel message and in empowering indigenous believers. As a matter of fact, many IGL barefoot pastors who are taking the gospel to unreached villages came to Christ through the work of Second Wave workers and churches.

Stories of the Second Wave

William Carey

William Carey, "the Father of Modern Missions," was a Second Wave pioneer in India. Carey was a man God used "for such a time as this." He grew up in England, apprenticing and working as a cobbler. Naturally curious and eagerly studious, he made time to learn the scriptures, to study botany, religions, and politics, and to master multiple languages. Carey came to Kolkata and settled there in 1793. His love of God, learning, language, and nature opened his eyes to see the image and hand of God in the people he encountered there.

Vishal Mangalwadi says in his book *The Legacy of William Carey*, "[Carey] saw India not as a foreign country to be exploited, but as his heavenly Father's land to be loved and saved…he believed in understanding and controlling nature instead of fearing, appeasing, or worshipping it, in developing one's intellect instead of killing it as mysticism taught. He emphasized enjoying literature and culture instead of shunning it…"

Based in respect and appreciation for his fellow image-bearers, Carey developed a set of objectives for the Mission he established in Serampore. They were fresh, powerful, and precocious in the midst of imperially ruled India. Those objectives stated:

1. Indians should lead any churches that were established.

2. While Indian churches could maintain fraternal relations with foreign church bodies, no overseas groups should impose control on the Indian churches.

3. Missionaries should esteem Indians and treat them as equals.

4. Serampore Mission will endeavor to develop Indian leadership.

Carey's passionate ideals were integral to the success of his work, and they were truly ahead of their time.

Raju Munisamy

In the mid-nineteenth century, India was still pocketed with royalty, and young Raju Munisamy's family were considered aristocracy. Despite his connections and comforts, Raju was an outlier and an extremely independent thinker. One evening during the early years of the Salvation Army's ministry in India, Raju walked past a street meeting and heard the gospel preached for the first time. He stopped and stayed. Standing on the streets of Chittoor that night, he gave his life to Jesus. Brimming with excitement and buoyed by a profound sense of freedom, Raju rushed home to tell his family what he had heard about the one true God and about what he had done. His parents were not happy.

So often, people movements begin among the marginalized, the outcasts, and those who have been oppressed or subjugated. As Christ was proclaimed in India, more often than not, those considered "untouchable" were the people who responded to God's love and grace. Raju's family, aghast that their son might be counted among these low people, put all their efforts into convincing him to recant. He would not. Soon, he got his hands on a Bible and started reading it around the house. The pressure was on. The entire family tried in every way to induce him to return to Hinduism. Still, he would not.

Not many weeks after Raju met Christ, his brother came to him privately before the evening meal, his face pale and strained. Quickly and quietly he warned Raju that their parents had poisoned his food. This was a huge blow to Raju. He realized that his parents would rather have him dead than to be dishonored by his "outcast" faith. Raju packed a few things and fled from his home. He came under the protection of the same English Salvation Army missionaries who had shared the gospel with him and given him his Bible. They convinced him to take on an alias, an English name, and he became Raju Stephens. If you haven't connected the dots yet, Raju Stephens is my great-grandfather. From that time on, Stephens was our family name. Each subsequent generation has come to know Christ and has stepped into his service, and it was my great-grandfather Raju who changed our family's legacy.

Raju Stephens, late 1940s

All of my great-grandparents were first-generation Christians, and from the time they gave their lives to the Lord, our family of faith has grown along with our earthly family. There is great enthusiasm among first-generation Christians. They believe that the most valuable, the most worthwhile thing in life, is to serve the Lord. Of course, that's the human side of things. On the other side—the more powerful side—is the Holy Spirit's call upon people's lives. Raju was independent and an outlier before he came to Christ, and the Lord used those bold, tenacious qualities for the Kingdom as he led Raju into service. My great-grandfather was ninety-six years old when he passed away, and until the very last months of his life, he was still working as an evangelist and an indigenous church planter.

In a sense, the focus on indigenous ministry in my spiritual family goes all the way back to Raju's early years as a Christian. As a young man, Raju refused to adopt the cultural mandates of the denominational missionaries. He wanted to be independent of those mandates, and he trusted the Lord's call on his life. My grandfather, Devaprasad Stephens, Raju's son, worked with Christian denominations for a time during his early years, but he developed a discomfort for the culturally irrelevant practices he saw imposed on the Indian church. Neither he nor his father viewed Western wineskins as vessels that would effectively carry the gospel across India. They dove headlong into building indigenous churches where the gospel could be preached in the people's heart languages. As such, these men had powerful platforms to proclaim the gospel, and they, along with their brothers and sisters, reaped an abundant harvest.

Second Wave Impact

Centuries of Second Wave Christian witness and ministry have made their mark in India. While I'll critique the ethos of the Second Wave and defend the need to move past it, I want to note how God used this wave during its season. Foremost, many people came to know Jesus Christ as Lord and savior during this Wave—my family included. Significant structures were put in place to educate new believers and to give many of them a measure of biblical literacy. An Indian Christian community was formed, and some denominations have been eager to be inclusive and to share power with their Indian brothers and sisters. In addition, the Western denominational structures provided longevity to the community and created a cohesiveness of the biblical message through the generations.

While Second Wave ministry paved the way for some of the tremendous church growth we are seeing now, parts of this wineskin continue to be barriers to an effective witness in India today. Western denominational power structures, created dependencies, and imported "one size fits all" frameworks are all vestiges of the Second Wave that linger today.

William Carey believed that overseas missions should not control Indian churches, but the truth is that they often still do. Generally, Western denominational structures continue to hold power and control in Second Wave churches. This is usually subtle and indirect. Many mission agencies are honestly intending to work toward partnership, but the nuances, intricacies, and tensions of partnerships and control make for difficult terrain. For example, created dependency is itself a control. If local Indian ministries are completely dependent on outside financial support, then that "privilege" correlates to a high level of control as to how that support is used.

I have turned down tens of thousands of dollars of support from a group that sought to fully fund one hundred churches in perpetuity. Why? It is not IGL's vision. In fact, it is detrimental to our vision. We eagerly work to establish churches that have learned to sacrificially give in support of their own fellowships. It is vital that the churches we plant are structured to become self-sustaining, self-replicating churches, growing in dependence on the Lord and becoming givers themselves.

Like I said, this Second Wave style of mission is often subtle, and even missionary agencies may not feel in control. They may feel controlled, in turn, by donors who say, "I have a lot of money for Project X that I'd like you to do, but if you decide to do Project Y, you won't get the money." A national organization may find itself in the position of doing Project X because there is funding, even though its leaders know and believe Project Y is more important. The question everyone has to wrestle with is: who should be defining and prioritizing the needs on the field?

If money and control go hand in hand, then certainly tradition and control do too. The larger and more established a ministry center is, the more likely it will operate under the "we've always done it this way, and we can't change it" paradigm. While today many people agree that indigenous ownership is effective and powerful, there is less agreement on how to work it out in real life when money and traditional institutions are in the mix.

I believe a bit of the problem in sharing our faith in contemporary India results from poor approaches the church has taken in the past. On one hand, non-Christians take a cynical view of even the best evangelical efforts: in Hindustan India, almost any Christian messaging is seen as a threat. On the other hand, there are truly problematic ways in which the church promotes and approaches conversion. I fear that many churches have not considered the barriers to the gospel message that they themselves are erecting. Attention-seeking megachurch activities and culturally insensitive approaches to evangelism have proved detrimental to the church's life and witness. Even language must be used with caution. Framing evangelism and witnessing as "crusades" or "campaigns," which make subtle connections to military tactics, can threaten hearers.

In contemporary India, politicians often accuse Christian missionary organizations and Christian non-governmental organizations (or NGOs) of converting people by coercion. Too often, those accusations are justified. For example, we are seeing prosperity gospel churches tie "conversion" to the extravagant "bait" of health and wealth. If the poorest of the poor are promised material wealth and comfort in exchange for conversion, isn't it very much like coercion? Physical and material gain take center stage, while introducing people to Jesus and his Good News for sinners fades into the background. Costi Hinn, himself a former prosperity preacher, said after a 2019 trip to India, "As the pastors shared their hearts, I was told that the entire region [southern India] is seeing a wave of compromise within the church. One pastor confessed that he has 'started preaching prosperity theology' because people will leave his church if he doesn't."

It is easier than ever for the church to copy and paste Western models, and increased exposure to Western media feeds this unhealthy trend. At present there is a "Hollywood" (or shall I say "Bollywood"?) glamour to televangelists. Young Indian leaders, especially the most charismatic, most gifted ones, are tempted to believe that they too can tap into megachurch crowds and popular acclaim if they simply do what they see on YouTube.

There are several specific "imported" frameworks that we see a lot these days. They initially have a big draw, but are significantly less effective than organic, layperson driven church growth. First, is the idea that "newer and bigger is better." Big buildings, new furnishings, famous preachers, Western music, a "churchy" atmosphere, and rave reviews about these things would seem to indicate whether a church is successful. God's perspective, however, is different. Isn't the Bible full of stories about little and insignificant things, which ultimately matter much in Kingdom economy? Think about salt and yeast, silently doing their work, but bringing about great results! Think of the Kingdom of God starting like a mustard seed and growing into substance and strength.

We must never measure our results or accomplishments based on a human scale. (How many people attend your church? How big is your building budget?) Kingdom results are measured differently: in changed lives, changed communities, loving lives, loving communities, individuals eager to share the Good News of Christ, and in communities whose greatest joy is to lift up his name.

Another problematic vestige of Second Wave ministry is the idea that "One Size Fits All." Efficiency is a high value in large, institutional bodies. It seems efficient to take what worked in one context and then impose it in every context. Ultimately, what appeared to be a streamlined growth process ends up *limiting* growth! Cookie-cutter methods fail to empower the church to take the unchanging message of the gospel and present it in ways that correspond to culture. They fail to see the distinct gifting profile of each local body of believers and to then energize those gifts in unique ways.

The Second Wave wineskin does not differ from any other wineskin in the fact that it has an expiration date. It is so easy, especially in institutional church models, to hold on for too long to the belief that yesterday's solutions will solve today's challenges. The church must remain a flexible and responsive organism, responsive not to culture but to *how God is working* in a specific culture.

God is working in India today, as he has been for millennia. Through all these years, the Lord has been preparing the church for a time when the desire for Indian cultural identity would reach a boiling point. Changes in the church and the present cultural uprising have come together in an electric moment for Indian Christianity. People are embracing a clear gospel message that is unencumbered by superimposed cultural trappings. Through this freedom, the Lord of the Harvest is, in fact, hastening the work. We are seeing people come to know him in unprecedented numbers, and we are seeing churches multiply and entire communities transformed.

We have learned much from both the First Wave and Second Wave of Christian ministry in India. By looking back at the past, we are able to glean understanding and wisdom for the future—a future where we can see and feel God's Spirit blowing in extraordinary ways, a future where we're tossing out old wineskins and replacing them with new ones. In the next chapter we will look at where and how God has been working in what I call The Third Wave of Christian ministry.

REFLECT

1. What things are we imposing that may be a barrier to the gospel? What are our "pants"?

2. Can you see ways that God is revealing himself within the culture of those we are trying to reach (millennials, Gen Z, etc.)?

3. What is in your current set of objectives for missions? Take a moment to write one or two based upon the example of William Carey's objectives. If you already have an updated set of objectives, is there anything you can learn or adjust from reading Carey's objectives?

4. What is the gifting profile in your local body of Christ?

CHALLENGE

"For though I am free from all men, I have made myself a slave to all, so that I may win more. To the Jews I became as a Jew, so that I might win Jews; to those who are under the Law, as under the Law though not being myself under the Law, so that I might win those who are under the Law; to those who are without law, as without law, though not being without the law of God but under the law of Christ, so that I might win those who are without law. To the weak I became weak, that I might win the weak; I have become all things to all men, so that I may by all means save some. I do all things for the sake of the gospel, so that I may become a fellow partaker of it" (1 Corinthians 9:19-23 NASB).

1. Based on the passage above, describe the ways Paul was willing to give up his cultural mandates in order to win more people to Christ.

2. Think about your own life and ministry. In what ways have you chosen to "become like" someone else for the sake of the gospel?

3. Dropping cultural mandates makes sense to us when we are thinking about missionaries moving from one country to another. There are also opportunities to reach a variety of people right in our own backyards. This may require us to drop some "micro" cultural mandates. For example, if the primary group of people you normally reach out to are middle-aged, married, and living in the suburbs, but God calls you to reach youth in the nearby high school, what "micro" cultural mandates would you need to drop in order to connect with those kids?

4. You may have to let go of some of your cultural mandates in order to effectively reach people with the gospel where you are right now. Think through who those groups of people might be and write them down. Start praying for these people groups (have others join you as well!) with the intention of having your heart open to the possibility of starting a study of the Bible with some of them.

KINGDOM VOICES

Gary Kinnaman
Pastor-at-Large, World Grace Church

This is the whole focus of ministry: How do we reproduce ourselves? How do we release the saints for the work of the ministry? How do we avoid getting institutionalized?

Author Peter Wagner said years ago that church planting is the best way to lead people to Christ and to make disciples. And we saw in our church, where I was pastor for twenty-five years, that the older we got, the bigger we got, the more it cost per person, per capita, to do ministry. And we also found that our first-time visitors were declining and the number of people who were coming to church was declining. As a new church, we'd had such momentum. It was totally a God thing; it was contagious.

But, you know, I believe that God moves on when we institutionalize. And that's one of the reasons I actually stepped down from my church. It was getting older and institutional. One day, I was on a plane coming back from Australia, and I was reading a book by Reggie McNeal. I felt that God was saying to me, "We can no longer make incremental changes; we have to make a fundamental change." And it took me about a year to realize that meant I needed to get out of the way, that I needed to make a change, that the church needed new leadership.

Jim Lyon
General Director, Church of God Ministries

In the States, there is a trend right now toward small church development. This is a discipling and church-planting motif. It's about the small group that meets at Starbucks or in the house meeting—the house church kind of thing. There really is a resonance toward that.

It's not pervasive, but it's really growing. In a new generation, there's a lot more traction for that kind of growing, and actually multi-sited churches are finding that is the first step towards new sites. Far-flung Starbucks meetups with young couples pretty soon become a part of the church, but they're functioning as a community of Christ out where they are. They don't come in anymore to the big hub.

I grew up in a world where I believed that the people who were closest to Jesus were the ones who were in the church building the most often. And I was one of those. I had people in my parish who only came on Sundays, but during the week they were active in the PTO, changing their local public school, and they truly were doing it for Jesus. I had to grow through my allegiance to the institutional church model to the salt and light model of Jesus.

Mission drift occurs when the church as an institution becomes the subject. I keep coming back to that truth because I come from a movement where the church was often the subject. The name of the church was so important. The organization of the church was so important. The music of the church was so important. All these things were church-oriented. And I grew up believing that if the name was right, then the church would be right. I don't think Jesus went to the cross for the name, Church of God. But when I was growing up, I thought so. Mission drift comes when the church as an institution becomes the center of attention, as if its success was the Kingdom's success.

Steve Moore
Former Executive Director of Missio Nexus, Executive Director of nexleader

We have some fairly strong cultural, and maybe even subliminal frameworks, for understanding what church is that don't apply when we talk about the global church. For example, if we were to talk about a church that's planted in rural India or the countryside of China or someplace in Africa and describe it as a group of Jesus followers with no formally trained leader (at least from an academic standpoint) who meet regularly under a tree behind someone's house to worship

Jesus and reflect on what it means to be a faithful disciple of Jesus, we wouldn't question the validity of that group as a church. But if we were to talk to someone here in the US who said, "I have a group of ten or twelve people that I meet with regularly in a Starbucks or in a park, and we meet regularly to study the Bible and talk about what it looks like to be a faithful disciple of Jesus," we would be reluctant to accept that as a church.

We have some pretty rigid cultural predispositions about what a church is here that don't apply to the rest of the world. The cultural expression of church in the North American context is not unbiblical, but it is extra-biblical. I go to a multi-site megachurch here in metro Atlanta; I have great relationships there; I'm part of a small group there; I find value in many of the things that we do. But almost nothing that we do is, in itself, rooted in the patterns of the New Testament church. That doesn't make it automatically bad. It's not necessarily unbiblical, but it is extra-biblical. The problem is, we have embraced that extra-biblical model without a willingness to ask hard questions about it. And so even when church leaders quietly admit that what we're doing is not consistently and predictably producing New Testament disciples, we keep doing it because it's the cultural framework that we've had.

Perhaps more problematic is when people experiment around the margins with forms of church that are actually probably more patterned after New Testament models of gatherings of believers in different homes and places and whatnot. We tend to view those as not just marginalized, but as something that is sub-optimal. It doesn't match the metrics that we have for success for a church. And I just find that to be a barrier to our thinking.

chapter 5

UNLEASH THE INDIGENOUS CHURCH

Chapter 5
Unleash the Indigenous Church

In the late 1990s, Sam Kumar set out from home for the Dharapurum Region of India. He was a Jesus follower and felt called by the Lord to take the gospel there. Despite knowing no one, he and his wife found a small hut in the town, settled in, and began to share their faith. They struggled. The work was off to a slow start. After a time, two people came to know the Lord. They joined Sam and his wife in the hut to pray and study the word of God. As they prayed and studied, the Spirit was moving. The four of them shared the gospel in faith, and neighbors and friends began to respond to Jesus.

By the time I met Sam Kumar in 2001, his house was filled with new believers, and they had run out of space. Recognizing the work of the Spirit, we rallied to build a Life Center for this new little church and for the surrounding community. India Gospel League provides Life Center spaces in communities where a church community is growing; these simple buildings provide space for a variety of community efforts including childcare, skill training, and church gatherings. Life Centers are typically 40 by 20 feet—or 800 square feet. That is about the size of two 2-car garages in an average Western home.

Sam Kumar was leading a church body that was motivated to prayerfully take the gospel out. In 2007, I received news that Sam had used his own money to add another 40 square feet to the Life Center, as they had once again run out of room. In 2010, I heard that he'd added another 30 square feet of space. And in 2012, he'd built on another 30 square feet.

Early on, Sam Kumar had joined our Vision 2000 community and caught the vision of planting churches all across India. At the same time that the Lord was adding numbers to the Dharapurum church, Sam and other believers from that community were going out to the surrounding villages with the gospel. As of today, they have planted fifteen churches in the region. With the aid of its partners, IGL has been able to provide Life Centers to three of these, and the remaining twelve villages have churches that have grown to the extent that they need a Life Center as well.

The Third Wave Is on the Move

Today, God is raising up equipped, committed, indigenous, disciple-making leaders across India, and he is using these faithful servants to ignite rural India for himself. Despite the odds and the many challenges, genuine church growth is outpacing anything we've seen in India before. In the last twenty-five years, millions of people living in rural India have embraced Christ. God is working through the unleashed church in this Third Wave of church growth to spread his Good News across the country.

THE THIRD WAVE
- Indigenous workers train local leaders
- Strategy is focused on empowering and equipping the church
- Churches are self-sustaining, reproducing, and life-giving
- The gospel explodes!

19th century   **present**

From our twenty-first-century vantage point, we see how God has laid a foundation for today's work. Now, after generations of restraint, the indigenous church has been released. An Indian Christian movement is happening here! The First and Second Wave of church growth paved the way for this fresh wave of ministry. God's Spirit is truly moving across India, changing the hearts and lives of its people and making them disciples and servants of his work!

My vision, and the vision of India Gospel League, is that we can come alongside these eager brothers and sisters to fan the flames. God's Kingdom will expand as we disciple, equip, and support them in their work, establish them in the word, and connect them to a network of indigenous resources. We are excited to move together into uncharted territory!

Building God's Kingdom, Not My Own

Very early in my ministry journey, God helped me make some shifts in how I thought about the work I was called to do. I served with my father in IGL and as a barefoot village pastor for about eleven years until 1988, when he passed away and I took on the leadership of the organization. It was relatively small then. Regardless, I was quite fearful of how I would lead this organization. How would I manage it? How would I run it? How would I raise the resources required to make everything work? Over the next year, through ups and downs, I became more comfortable managing, funding, and leading all of the day-to-day operations. Soon I was asking how I could *grow* the organization. My prayer was, "Lord, I want India Gospel League to grow. I want to see churches in every state."

At that time, IGL only had churches in one state, my home state of Tamil Nadu. And so we started a training center—a Bible school to train young people. We selected the most talented and most skilled people we could find, and we put them into training and then sent them out into the villages. It seemed like a great idea: train the best and send them out to share the gospel and plant churches where it was received. This is how we got started in those early days of trying to grow the ministry.

Over the next two years, however, the Lord started bringing people into my life who I would never have imagined as church planters. All kinds of people from every segment of society were encountering Jesus. They were so full of zeal and excitement that they were instinctively sharing the gospel with their families, friends, and communities. They simply couldn't help but talk about what God was doing in their lives. God was busy raising indigenous people—nearly all of them new believers—as church planters. I just didn't know it yet. It really shouldn't have surprised me that God would work this way, but it did!

These new believers would have ten to fifteen people gathered together somewhere (under a tree or packed into a house), studying the word, sharing whatever the Holy Spirit was revealing to them, and singing songs composed from verses they'd read in the Bible. What would you call that? I may have been a little slow to realize it, but, of course, we'd call that a *church*! These eager believers didn't even know that they were planting churches! Churches were being formed organically through the witness of the gospel message and the power of the Holy Spirit.

One after another, the Lord started bringing these people into my life. I spent a lot of time with these sweet servants, praying with them, encouraging them, and teaching them. They had no affiliation, they had no friends, and they had no financial support. They were all alone, just called by the Lord, witnessing and planting churches in their villages. They didn't even know that they were planting churches, so we had to tell them. What a privilege to deliver that message!

This movement of the Spirit happened for a couple of years, and by 1990, about one hundred and fifty young believers gathered together, eager to be equipped and supported in the work that they *were already* doing. God was up to something amazing and unprecedented. He challenged our status quo and was doing something that had never happened in our sphere of ministry before. As I was watching all of it unfold, I had to be honest with myself: I had been trying to do my own thing. I wanted to train up the "best and brightest" to build *my own* organization, to plant *my own* churches, to start *my own* institution. I wanted to be present everywhere. I wanted to stand on a pedestal. I wanted people to say, "There's the hero who's winning India for Christ!"

But God changed my heart. He said, "Your call is not to build an empire; your call is to build the Kingdom of God." I'm an Indian pastor. I'm the product of generations of Indian Christians. I'm not a First Wave or Second Wave missionary. Yet I, too, had to learn that I am not called to become a hero. I am not called to build my own church. I am called to build God's Kingdom. And this Kingdom is made up of hundreds and thousands of individual believers and small communities of believers who are all working out their faith, together, before the Lord.

Today, IGL is not a denomination. It is not a command center. It exists to train, support, encourage, empower, and facilitate the missional community of ordinary believers whom God is raising up in India from among the masses.

Three Dynamics of the Unleashed Church

Over the years, I've observed several ways in which the Holy Spirit moves in the unleashed, fresh, Third Wave church. I want to share these dynamics with you to celebrate what God is doing in the indigenous church in India and so you can share our hope that God can work like this anywhere in the world, if people's hearts are soft and willing!

1. In the unleashed church, every believer is an evangelist.

Today in India, the "of the people, for the people" church-planting movement reflects the kind of growth in the first-century church. Every single person is involved in multiplication. There is no divide between clergy and laity; rather, pastors believe their job is to "equip the saints for the work of ministry, for building up of the body of Christ" (Ephesians 4:12 ESV). I submit to you that the intentional, intrinsic, organic growth of the New Testament church shows not just a way that church growth can happen; it also shows the way that a strong, sustainable, bottom-up witness develops in a community and moves out from there.

In our village churches, there aren't standalone church-planting pastors starting new churches autonomously. Pastors may be facilitators who give direction and mobilize workers, but in reality, it's the church that is multiplying itself! The church has to be self-multiplying. It cannot become inward-focused. It's got to reach out to the community and give life to the community. That is the mission of the church. Each believer is stepping out into his or her sphere of influence and is being used by the Lord as an agent of change.

When a person comes to Christ, even before he or she is baptized, we encourage that believer to share their story of faith with one other person. There's nothing theological or biblical about it, but we view sharing with others to be part of their growth and discipleship. We don't wait for new believers to become fully equipped, to know everything about theology, or to have all of their doctrines memorized. From day one, they're encouraged, empowered, and equipped to witness to their own people, to share the gospel with them, and to teach them what they know. This way, when they are baptized, their own disciples are standing with them and celebrating. Praise God!

2. In the unleashed church, every Christian is a Kingdom builder, and young people are significant contributors.

People often say that young people are the next generation's leaders. This statement sounds good, but what are the young people to do in the meantime? When we don't consider youth as contributors, when we keep them out of sight, pacified, and entertained, or when we hold them back until they are "ready" to serve, we are pouring water on fire.

Praveen

God began to form my value for young leaders long ago with my friend Praveen. I met Praveen when he was a young, inexperienced, zealous man. He was newly married, and he and his wife were regular attendees at a Bible study for high school and college-aged students. One evening after the study, he approached me. I could see immediately that something was wrong because Praveen was almost in tears. I took him aside and asked what was going on. He blurted out, "I cannot win any older people! I have led young people to Christ, and I am discipling them, but I cannot win any adults! We are all too young!"

I was taken aback by his tears and concern, but I asked him to tell me more. I found out that Praveen was meeting regularly with twenty—yes, twenty—young people whom he had introduced to the Lord. They were getting together every Sunday to study the Bible. The trouble in Praveen's mind was that he really wanted to be a church planter, and obviously he couldn't plant a church of only teenagers.

"Why not?" I challenged him. "Does the Bible say how old a person must be to plant a church? Does the Bible state any sort of an age requirement for the people in a church? The truth is, if you have a group of twenty people gathered to study, worship, and fellowship, then you've got yourself a church! And if everyone in that church is a teenager, then you've got yourself a young church! Young, and full of potential."

Praveen was still concerned, though. He wanted to know how he would get any elders to help lead the church. I looked at him and said, "You will raise up your elders." I discipled Praveen, and he continued to lead the church that he had planted without knowing that he had planted it. He nurtured men who could become elders. He taught them the word, showed them what leadership looked like, and helped them operate in their gifting. Today, Praveen oversees a network of forty-two reproducing and life-giving churches that are all generations of that first, very young, church plant. Thirty full-time church-planting pastors have been raised and trained from among these churches.

So are young people the next generation's leaders? I think it's better to say that young people are *this* generation's leaders. They are the ones who set the trends, who are making the wheels turn, who zealously pour out their lives for the church. They are setting godly courses for their own lives and are influencing the little children—the true next generation. It is through the zeal and love of so many young people that the foundation of the future church is emerging in our country. It is through their faithful service that even more people are becoming rooted in the word and in what it looks like to live out faith.

Praveen

Now, let's talk specifics for a moment. It is very important that we establish new believers in the word. It is essential because so many of them come from the dark and syncretistic background of Hinduism and other tribal religions. They need to understand what they believe in and be able to communicate their faith effectively. That's how the church becomes sustainable. To that end, this year we will have had over 965,000 children enrolled in our Children's Gospel Club program, which we have been hosting for twenty-one years. Children's Gospel Clubs are similar to Vacation Bible School in the States, with multiple village churches hosting clubs for kids in their area. Unlike a typical VBS one-week experience, Children's Gospel Clubs are ongoing, week after week. Upwards of 18,000 young people who are new believers themselves staff the clubs.

Is this scandalous? Dangerous? Unwise? Sure, there are inherent challenges, but we are so grateful that new believers are the ones discipling these little children. So why do we do this, and how does it work? Well, in order to teach these children, our new believers must first be taught. They must read the Bible, they must learn the stories and their meaning, and then they must give away what they've been given. They immediately learn that the Christian life is not about being a taker but about being a sacrificial giver. We give them the immediate opportunity to be involved in practical ministry within the context of the local church. No believer—not even the young—who comes to faith in the church is made to feel comfortable sitting there and being entertained. Rather, we invest our energy in helping each one to stand up and take his or her place in the body of Christ.

3. A high investment in organic, relational discipleship permeates the first two dynamics of the unleashed church.

Inseparable from the call to "go," the worldwide church is called to discipleship. Jesus said to "go and make disciples" (Matthew 28:19 NIV). That's what we do as we go, wherever we go! It doesn't matter whether a church is being established in an American suburb or in a rural village in the mountains of India. Jesus showed us and told us it would be through this intimate, intentional "caught and taught" instruction that his people would learn to walk in and follow his footsteps.

It would be inaccurate to talk about the call of discipleship without also making clear that it is a challenge to carry out. It is difficult. Discipleship takes time, patience, intentionality, responsiveness, and a willingness to wade into messy situations. It requires real love, sourced in and fueled by the person of Jesus. The challenges of making disciples may vary from East to West, and even from person to person, but the fruit of investment is the same. At IGL, we are very intentional about making any program or activity we do subservient to the goal of growing a strong church through discipleship. We know that out of this, a healthy, vibrant, sustainable, and dynamic church will emerge which is able to purposefully and powerfully carry out its redemptive mission in this world.

No matter how extensive, evangelistic efforts and preaching alone will never result in the kind of effective discipleship central to the Great Commission. Discipleship requires time. It requires real relationships— living life together and doing ministry side by side. It requires intentionality and a framework; it will neither happen by itself nor in a void. Relationships within the local church are the framework for effective discipling, where believers are equipped to live lives worthy of the gospel, for evangelism, and for further discipling. Consider 2 Timothy 2:2, where the apostle Paul exhorts his spiritual son Timothy saying: "The things you have heard me say in the presence of many witnesses entrust to reliable people who will also be qualified to teach others" (NIV). Without robust, organic discipleship, the rapidly growing Indian church will become reliant on paid clergy. Without discipleship, we will see the same fault lines between "workers" and "pew-sitters" that have evolved in the Western church over the years.

At a core level, organic discipleship relationships are the material from which organic, responsive, unleashed churches are built. These churches have scripture study in their DNA. They have corporate prayer in their DNA. They have real-time responses built into their DNA. They are agile yet grounded. Isn't it clear that this is the church that we need today? And even more profoundly, isn't this the church of the book of Acts, the church that God intended?

One of the challenges of a discipleship-DNA church is that cellular level growth is incremental and, by nature, slow. For instance, over the recent years, many thousands of Dalits (whom you may know as "untouchables") have come to the Lord. New converts from among this population are still coming into the church in waves. And, by all accounts, this is amazing! However, conversion and discipleship cannot be separated. Conversion happens in a moment and is exciting and sometimes public. Discipleship is quiet, happens over a long period of time, and is difficult. As such, we may be tempted to disconnect the two or de-emphasize discipleship.

There is much more harvest to bring in, but in so many ways it must be reaped quietly and without fanfare. This "silent revolution" is critical for the long-term future of the church in India. That is why evangelism and discipleship cannot be separated one from the other. They are not either/or propositions. They are not a balancing act. They work together. As Dalits come to the Lord, they are also being discipled and are growing into hundreds of strong, flexible church plants.

The bottom line—the need of the hour now—is to ensure that indigenous, rural churches are equipped to meet the challenges that face them individually and as parts of the larger church. Strategic, multi-level, systematic discipleship, including the teaching and training of every willing believer, is the key. Believers must learn that ministry is not just sowing and reaping but building wisely and incrementally upon a firm foundation. It can only happen with a long-term perspective, a long-term commitment, and a deep reliance on the power of the Holy Spirit.

Three Keys to Unleashing the Indigenous Church

We've explored what the Third Wave unleashed church looks like from a philosophical standpoint, but what does it look like in practice? As I've watched churches start with just a few people and grow into much larger gatherings, I've noticed that some churches thrive while others struggle to get their feet under them. So what does it take to make a church strong at its very core? In my opinion, there are three key things church leaders must do—or not do. Let's dig into these now.

1. Turn Around—See Where God Is Working

Ready? Set? Press pause. Yes, the first key in unleashing the church is to stop what you're doing. Put aside what you're planning. Set down your agenda and look to see where God is working. Do you want to experience the release of his Spirit in your life and ministry? Then look to see where God is working and invest there. The truth is, such a turn from our own plans and agendas requires spiritual intervention. Then it requires repentance.

In Matthew 3:2 and 4:17, we see John the Baptist and Jesus respectively calling people to "repent, for the Kingdom of heaven is at hand" (ESV). Of course, repent, or *metanoia*, simply means "to turn around," and we most often interpret this as a turning away from sin. In the calls of Jesus and John in Matthew's letter, though, it is important to notice where the people were to reorient themselves— specifically, *to whom* they were to reorient themselves. The Kingdom had come! Jesus was there. God was at work among them. But the people's hearts were solidly focused on traditional religion and religious institutions. God was there among them, and they were missing it! Repent. Turn around. See what Jesus is doing.

Certainly, there are times when we feel that this whole "where God is working" is not so clear cut. We may feel a bit confused. As we're told in Matthew 11, there came a day when John the Baptist wasn't so sure that Jesus was really "the one." John was in prison and, from that vantage point, was a little less certain that the Kingdom had actually come. Jesus sent "turning around words" to John— reorienting words. He instructed his disciples, "Go back and report to John what you hear and see: The blind receive sight, the lame walk, those who have leprosy are cleansed, the deaf hear, the dead are raised, and the Good News is proclaimed to the poor" (Matthew 11:4–5 NIV). Turn around, John. God is here, and he is at work.

Do you remember the tail end of the "woman at the well" story in the book of John? It's kind of funny. The disciples return from a little grocery shopping to find Jesus talking with a Samaritan woman. John takes pains to tell us that "no one asked" Jesus anything about this unusual conversation. Instead, they went right into a conversation about dinner. The disciples urged Jesus to eat. He told them he had food they didn't know about. They wondered who might have delivered it. Jesus interrupts, doing his best to turn them around, to reorient them. "Open your eyes and look at the fields! They are ripe for harvest" (4:35 NIV).

Open your eyes. Look. There's a harvest. Jesus drilled down into this a bit more, telling them that this harvest was ready right now, but not because of their own hard work. God had prepared the soil and the seed for that moment. Open your eyes. Look. See where God is working. Then go reap the harvest.

So, instead of focusing on "the way it's always been," instead of fixating on "what's for dinner tonight," take a look around to see what God has been up to. This is a massive turning of the ship. It won't be accomplished without repentance and submission to a good, powerful God who is more than able to build his church. *His* church.

As I shared earlier, the first dramatic shift in my ministry philosophy came when the Lord called on me to repent of my empire mindset. He turned me around to nurture a Kingdom mindset. The scripture describes this paradigm: "He must increase, but I must decrease" (John 3:30 ESV). The church is unleashed as we step off center stage.

2. Raise Up the Right People

We must see where God is working, and we must see with whom God is working. The second key in unleashing the church is to raise up the right people. While not always true, this is often most effective when it happens from the bottom up rather than from the top down.

It is very easy to look at the best of the people you see and say, "He or she will be my hero. Surely this gifted, strong, put-together person will be the one through whom God wants to work!" But to do this without regard for who it is that God is choosing is banking on our human wisdom. What about the powerhouse of God's wisdom? One of my heroes is pastor Daniel. I wish that I could introduce you to him, although it might make you feel a little uncomfortable. You see, Pastor Daniel's face is disfigured by leprosy. He also doesn't have fingers, as they were eaten up by the disease and fell from his hands. But Daniel is a man of God.

Daniel, Sam, and Daniel's wife, Esther

I met Daniel twenty years ago when he was living on the streets. At this time, leprosy was even more prevalent in India than it is now, and we were reaching out to people with leprosy by providing regular meals and medical care. Daniel started coming in to get food, and that's how I got to know him. Of course, sharing the gospel was woven into everything that we were doing, and we regularly talked about the gospel message during the meals. Daniel heard the message, and the Lord captured his heart. From then on, we became close. Daniel never asked for anything. If I asked what he needed, he would say, "I don't want anything. I am happy now because I have Jesus." Even so, he was one of the first people for whom we built a home because he had been living on the streets.

Daniel and his wife set up house, and three times a day, they set aside time to pray together, sing, and worship the Lord. Now, homes in Indian villages are very close to one another, and they don't typically have windows or doors that close tightly. Windows are usually open, safeguarded by colorful, sturdy, decorative iron grates. Indoors and outdoors, private and public, blend together. Neighbors hear everything. They see everything. Daniel's neighbors were hearing and seeing. And pretty soon, they started asking questions. "You have nothing in life," they said. "You are a leper. Why are you so happy?" Of course, Daniel was thrilled to have an opportunity to answer that question, and as he answered, he led several people to the Lord. None of these new believers were lepers. None of his neighbors were. Purposely, we'd built Daniel's home, not isolated in a leper colony, but in the middle of "everyone else." And people were intrigued.

The next time Daniel came to get a meal, he said, "Pastor, thank you for building this home for me. Several people have come to the Lord!" This was wonderful news! "Praise the Lord!" I said. We prayed together, and he left. At the next meal, Daniel said, "Pastor, thank you for building a home for me. But now I have a problem." My heart sank. What could have happened in such a short time? Daniel continued, "Now there are sixty people gathering in my home to learn about Jesus, and we have run out of room." Then, for the first time, Daniel asked for something. "I hate to ask you," he ventured, "I don't like to ask," he went on, "but would you build a church building for us?" Once he had gotten that first request out of the way, another quickly followed. "I'm sharing everything I know about the Bible. I'm telling them anything I've learned from you, but we would like someone to come and teach us *more*."

The house of Daniel the leper was filled beyond capacity by neighbors who had heard and seen Jesus in his life. Daniel and his wife were praying for the people who came in more needy and broken on the inside than Daniel the leper was on the outside. They prayed for healing, and people were healed—inside and out. And yes, Daniel got his church building. As a matter of fact, an American church got to participate in this work of God. They had provided the funds for Daniel's house, and when asked, they eagerly gave again in order to build a Life Center and to bring an indigenous pastor into Daniel's village. Daniel got his wish: he was being taught and discipled, and he was able to teach and disciple too.

Today, Daniel himself has planted over fifteen churches. The village where he lives, and where the Life Center was established, is thriving! Two or three small industries are in full swing, the economy has grown, the original church is flourishing, and people from that church have planted three or four more churches in neighboring villages. God took what Daniel had—a small home and a huge heart, brimming with gratitude for Jesus—and used them powerfully.

Have you heard of Daniel before? I didn't think so. In a world of big names, true heroes tend to be anonymous. Let's ask God to give us eyes to see where he is working and in whom he is working. Let's raise up the right people.

Far too often, we believe that leadership is based on credentials earned in classrooms or upon titles bestowed in ceremonies. This belief, perpetuated by the institution of the church over the centuries, has been a grave mistake and has done little to grow God's Kingdom. What we've failed to understand is that biblical leadership is not *assigned* so much as it is *recognized*. If we want to change the world, we should invest in people who are *already* changing the world. These are people who are doing God's work at the grassroots level: in their homes, at work, in their communities, in their churches. Our challenge is to "see" them and then to come alongside them, encouraging and empowering them.

What do you think this looks like in your church? What unnecessary barriers might there be between eager workers and significant roles in the church? Are you and your team willing to evaluate this? Does your church have the relational ties necessary to discover who is about Kingdom business in their everyday lives? It can be difficult to "see" people who are about the business of the Kingdom, especially if they are not doing it *our way* or in *our building*. Perhaps we see them stepping out to serve, but they're doing it "wrong" or with a healthy dose of immaturity. I'll submit an old adage: "It's easier to contain a raging fire than to heat up a cold stone." In other words, if there is zeal for the Lord, excitement about his grace, and love for the lost, we can work with that! Yes, this person may need to have some rough edges smoothed. They may need to become diligent in their study of the scriptures. They may need to learn some sophisticated ways of interacting with controversial topics. But thank God for that fire in their heart! I'd rather work with a rough but fired-up believer any day of the week! A sophisticated, worldly-wise, Bible-smart person whose heart is cold toward the Lord will be greatly limited in his ability to accomplish anything significant in God's Kingdom.

3. Leaders, Stop Doing Everything.

That brings me to the third key in unleashing the indigenous church: *leaders, stop doing everything*. The idea that only paid staff do the work of the church is a vestige of the clergy-laity divide. While we may have put that aside philosophically or in our written statements, it is difficult to put aside in practice, don't you think? As leaders and as disciplers, our job is not to do everything for everyone but rather to equip the saints for works of service (Ephesians 4). I realize that I'm not telling you anything that you don't already know. Perhaps what I'm saying is this: Do it. Cut the cord. Step back. Leave an uncomfortable space that someone else needs to fill. It will be awkward and messy. Failure will be noticeable. Many things will not be done the way that you'd envisioned. But can you not still support work that is not done just the way that you would do it?

Let me share an example of how this challenge might look. I told you about my family in the last chapter. Ever since my great-grandfather, Raju Munisamy, came to Christ, our family's hearts have been alive with the desire to see the indigenous church unleashed. It seems there is a strong, independent streak in our DNA. (And yes, sometimes that gets us into trouble!) But the Lord has shaped that streak and used it mightily for his purposes. When my father was a young, fiery, passionate servant of the Lord, God granted him great success as an indigenous worker. He started schools, created homes for orphaned children, and planted many churches. Through this effort, two to three thousand people came to the Lord. God had granted him effectiveness.

Of course, during that time, in the 1940s and '50s, the Second Wave was alive and well. Many Western missionaries were on the ground in India, working with Indian believers under the structure of their Western denominations. My father came into contact with a woman from such a denomination. I've always known her as "Mother Eaton." As a denominational missionary, she had a lot in her pocket: collateral, connections, tradition, and the allure of anything Western. Emma Eaton could easily have taken note of my father's charisma and drive and sought to shape him into a model subsidiary of her denominational work. But unlike many missionaries of Second Wave ministry, she did not. She saw that the Lord had positioned my dad in a place of effectiveness, and she wanted to work where God was working. Rather than stepping in to shape or to control, she met my dad as an equal. She supported his work and used the tools in her pocket as a partner, not as a boss.

This relationship could not have been without bumps in the road, differences of opinion, or the diminishment that naturally comes as we lift others up. But because Mother Eaton did not try to "do everything" in her role as a leader, she was able to create space to support a work that resulted in a much greater yield.

Even when we are ready to try out the increase/decrease dynamic of Kingdom economy, the rubber eventually meets the road over one ubiquitous issue: control. It is a normal human tendency to want to be in control of every situation. We want to determine where we need to go, we want to plan every detail, and we want to decide where we're going and how we'll get there. Even if we've begun to move from control to collaboration, it's certain that the Lord will take us on a journey to purify our hearts over this issue. He will remind us that he is the Creator and we are not. He will show us that even the control that we *think* we have we do not have. He is sufficient, not needy. He does not require our best achievements. He wants us to see how beautiful it is when the diverse body of Christ rallies together, each using his or her own gift, working where God is working, depending on him for everything!

I'm so grateful that God corrects our ideas of who is in charge, of who "the heroes" of his story really are.

Diverse Church Planters and Women Leaders

Today IGL is working with more than 6,900 church planters who commit to planting one church every year and who are empowering those churches to multiply themselves. God has helped us to plant over 100,000 churches in the past thirty years, and it's because we gave up control. We said "God, do your work." Giving up control means recognizing that every church does not have to be the same, that cookie-cutter style churches are not ideal. Giving up control means we celebrate believers expressing faith in their own cultural packaging.

In 1998, we started an organization called the Non-Denominational Association of Interdependent Churches, or NAIC. I know it's a long and complicated acronym, but don't laugh; it's intentional! You see, we don't want to go back in history to a framework that emphasizes expediency, management, and control. Our message is not, "Do it this way!" No. We want to emphasize that these churches are unique, culture specific, and interdependent. They maintain their uniqueness even as they come together around God's call.

Village churches do whatever they want, as long as they are witnessing and multiplying. They may fold their hands in worship or lift their hands in worship. They may meet outside or in a building. Regardless of what they do and how they do it, the "wine" (spiritual life) is alive, organic, bubbling with vitality, and of central importance. The "wineskin" can change any time as needed. It can be blue, yellow, pink—it doesn't matter—as long as it does a good job of carrying the wine.

Interestingly, the work of the church, which is to carry and share the wine, is most effective when we depend on one another to do the work—when we do the work together. No one can do it by themselves. In fact, we need each other! We need each other to fulfill God's Kingdom purposes in our churches and communities.

Also in 1998, IGL asked local pastors to identify women in their congregations who were already giving their lives in service to the Lord. Our vision was to come alongside these women to encourage, enable, and equip them in the work they were doing. We called this movement "Women with a Mission."

In history and around the world, women have often been subjugated and considered second-class. Today, women in India are sadly still the "least of these." In 2018, a Reuters poll found India to be "the most dangerous country for women." They suffer abuse in their homes, are less likely to receive an education, have inadequate access to health care, are subject to threats of sex trafficking, and face general discrimination because of their gender. As a result of their position in society, many carry with them a deep sense of inadequacy and helplessness. Yet, we recognize that these are daughters of God who have significance in his Kingdom! Today, there are 5,620 women gathering in local groups to be discipled and equipped for Kingdom work. They are preaching the gospel, strengthening their local churches, discipling younger women, and leading programs dedicated to village flourishing.

Isn't God's economy beautiful? The needy become gift givers, the least of these are positioned as contributors, and each see their own value and view their work as contributing to the value of another. As we look to see where God is working, invest in raising up the right people (no matter their denomination or gender), and collaborate rather than control, we find our investment multiplied exponentially!

The Unleashed Church Is Focused on the Great Commission

Before we move on, I want to dig in to one last critical characteristic of the unleashed church: outward focus (or the Great Commission). Outward focus is a core strand of the Christian's DNA, but I am concerned that this strand is being subtly diminished and altered. If we do not tend to it, we will find that "go into all the world" has been redefined to mean something quite different from what Jesus intended. Already I have heard "go into all the world" redefined as social justice and reduced to raising one's own family well. It almost seems as if the distinctives of an unleashed church (every believer a Kingdom builder, low control/high investment, relational discipleship) have become unique and countercultural.

It is worth noting that as the Western church struggles, it is also becoming more and more countercultural for churches to focus on the Great Commission. Of course, there are the outsized examples of churches that have built bowling alleys, who sip lattes at Starbucks-quality coffee bars, and who are entertained by fog machines and laser shows. More commonly, though, as I travel the States, I interact with churches who acknowledge that God is working in India, but they are not interested in supporting this work. They feel exclusively called to their own communities. It is an insidious perspective, one that seems to indicate that we can only respond to part of God's call on our lives and not the whole of it.

Social justice is important, and investing in one's own family is important, but we are not in an either/or situation. Doing one good thing does not replace the call Jesus has made on every Christian and on his church to go into all the world. Why do we tend to frame it this way? Are we afraid that if we invest "outside" that our own growth will be stunted? The truth is that the church is not stunted but unleashed when we cultivate an outward-focused DNA.

Earlier we talked about God's economy in terms of increase and decrease. A second distinctive of God's economy is that as we pour ourselves out to tend to the flourishing of others, we actually become more and more vigorous and fruitful. A new believer with a captured heart looks like a person who organically, exuberantly, and confidently shares the Good News with others. It follows, then, that a community captured by Jesus will also be turned outward, eager to walk others out of the darkness and into the light.

If tending to the flourishing of others is part of a Kingdom distinctive, then in contrast, "personal empire building" must be a distinctive of the flesh. You and I know the draw of gathering fruit to fill our own storehouses, stockpiling resources, and dreaming of "bigger and better" buildings, curricula, slideshows, and sound systems. But unencumbered pouring into self is a fast track to stagnation. The classic example is that of the Dead Sea—a sea brimming with nutrients, but because it has no outlet, it accumulates too much of the "good stuff." Specifically, the Dead Sea accumulates salt and therefore becomes toxic to life.

Both the Dead Sea and the Sea of Galilee are sourced from the same place—the Jordan River—but have little else in common. The Sea of Galilee is beautiful, teeming with fish, and home to a variety of wildlife. The Dead Sea is quite literally a dead end. Over one million tons of water evaporate from the closed system of the Dead Sea every day. What a waste!

When communities become inwardly focused, hoarding what they've been given instead of stewarding, then even what they've been given evaporates. This kind of inward, toxic, dead environment is a sure result of what coauthors Peter Greer and Chris Horst refers to as "mission drift" in their book by the same name. Greer says in an interview with Matt Smethurst of The Gospel Coalition, "We chose the word *drift* intentionally. It has the image of slowly, silently, and with little fanfare carrying away to a new destination. It's not dramatic, and yet anyone who's spent time on a boat of any size knows it happens."

No one can argue that *the* mission of the church is to make disciples of the nations, baptizing them and teaching them to obey everything that Jesus taught. Yet when almost half of American millennials believe that it's wrong to share their faith, it seems that the "drift" has evolved to a full "abandon ship."

But before we move on, I'd like to take a moment to acknowledge how mightily God is unleashing the most unlikely people in the most unlikely place to build the Kingdom of God. Honestly, when I hear the stories of some of the people who came to Christ and are sharing the Good News with others, I can't help but think of Jesus' disciples—the most ragtag group one could imagine. It's funny how God still works in the same way, isn't it? Calling the lost and lonely, the unlikely and unworthy, and redeeming them to himself and his work of spreading the Good News. Just like Jesus' disciples, we are called to deny ourselves, take up our cross, and follow him. This is where we find our greatest freedom. This is when we are truly unleashed to serve others and build God's Kingdom here on earth.

REFLECT

1. How many people in your congregation take on roles in God's work? Is most of the work of your church done by paid staff, or does a significant percentage of your whole congregation participate in raising up others to be workers in the Kingdom of God?

2. If people are generally not mobilized, take some time to think about why this might be. What unnecessary barriers might exist? What would it look like to unleash the people of God in your fellowship?

3. If God calls you to "decrease" for his mission, do you trust him enough to do that? What might that look like in your life? Consider this example: what ministry responsibilities do you have that you could delegate to other, younger believers? Where is the Lord asking you to give (or "shift") your control over to him?

CHALLENGE

1. *"Repent, for the Kingdom of heaven is at hand" (Matthew 3:2 ESV).*

   John the Baptist called people to repent (change their direction) in response to Jesus' presence. Ask God if there are places where you need to "turn around" in order to see where he is actively working.

2. *So we have not stopped praying for you since we first heard about you. We ask God to give you complete knowledge of his will and to give you spiritual wisdom and understanding. Then the way you live will always honor and please the Lord, and your lives will produce every kind of good fruit. All the while, you will grow as you learn to know God better and better (Colossians 1:9–10 NLT).*

   Pray a prayer like this one of Paul's regularly, because spiritual wisdom and understanding can only be given to us by God. We need spiritual vision to see where God is working. Keep an eye out for what he shows you! This prayer is one that God loves to answer.

3. *Jesus told them, "Go back to John and tell him what you have heard and seen—the blind see, the lame walk, those with leprosy are cured, the deaf hear, the dead are raised to life, and the Good News is being preached to the poor" (Matthew 11:4–5 NLT).*

When John the Baptist is hurting and confused, Jesus provides him with reassurance. He points to evidence of his transforming hand. What have you "heard and seen?" Does it give you any insight as to where God is working around you? Is it in a younger age group? Is it through a service ministry? Is it far away in rural India? Will you take him up on his leading?

KINGDOM VOICES

Becky Stanley
Director of Children's Ministries, India Gospel League

Meeting people at their point of need—that's discipleship. That's what I see as discipleship. Discipleship means reading the Bible, understanding the scriptures, and living that scripture out alongside Jesus. It's not, "Okay, so here are some of the things that I've learned from the Bible. Now let me go do it." No. It's, "How do I live my life with Jesus, in my context, in the power of the Holy Spirit?"

In India as a new Christian, you're ostracized. As a new Christian, you face all kinds of persecution. As a new Christian, you have so much unlearning to do, and you can be misunderstood. So you accept these truths: I cannot do this by myself. I cannot go and talk to people in another caste. I cannot abstain suddenly from going to the temple. I cannot stay away from eating the temple food. How do I handle these situations? Who do I turn to? Jesus. He's walking on the road, and I have to walk with him, and when I do, he will bring these answers to my life.

Somebody beautifully explained what following Jesus looks like. They said that the disciples, the ones that followed closer to Jesus, were the ones that had more dust on their feet because they were always running and trying to catch up. Their feet were dirtier and dustier because they had to keep up with the master. So I think discipleship is in a way like that. You're following your master so closely because you want to live life with him—in the journey that he's taking you on, not on your journey.

So, it's not just head knowledge. It's not just compassionate acts of service. It's not just a formula. No. It's a way of life that is totally surrendered. I don't know how else to say it. The way Paul says it is, "I have been crucified with Christ. It is no longer I who live, but

Christ who lives in me" (Galatians 2:20 ESV). This is the life of a disciple. And that's what we try to engage our new believers in, telling them, teaching them, "Yes, you come to conferences, you study God's word, you have to understand who Jesus is—his nature, his teachings, his principles, his idea of life." In all of that, you learn, you understand, but the head knowledge has to translate to the heart. And even then, both the head and the heart have to completely surrender and live that crucified life. That's discipleship for us.

Dave Ferguson
Bestselling Author and Founding and Lead Pastor of Chicago's Community Christian Church

I see churches in Africa and India do discipleship way better than we do in the States. Either because of cultural forces or because they can't afford to go out and buy a church building like we do in the West, they stick to the biblical principle—we're going to develop more disciples. And some of them have leadership gifts or apostolic evangelistic gifts, and then they go out and start communities that do the same thing, called churches. In the States, I think we've kind of disconnected the two things. And a couple of things happen: On the church planting side, because we predominantly have a "launch large" strategy of church planting, you can become a multi-site church if you grow a successful church in the suburbs, because people will give enough money. Then you can throw a half million dollars at it and start another church. And if you do that five or six times, it is, I guess, reproducing. And I think that's a good thing. It's just not a *great* thing. And it's not multiplication, it doesn't get you the movement.

With the India Gospel League, believers have a clear understanding that discipleship happens "life on life"; oftentimes in the West, our understanding is that discipleship has more to do with cognitive content or trying to take people through a curriculum or through a class. And then if they go through this class with a set number of weeks of content, then they've been discipled. We don't tell them, "It's life on life, then you do it with somebody else, and they do it with somebody else."

Reggie McNeal
Missional Leadership Specialist, Leadership Network

There are folks who say, "Yeah, you know, this Kingdom stuff's good. But when do we get people to the church?" Jesus established the church to get people to the Kingdom, not the other way around. The church is not the destination; the Kingdom is. And some folks in church as an institution struggle with this wider bandwidth of church expression because it doesn't fit the categories that we've developed. We want to wrap it in biblical language and theological stuff, and we develop this classification of clergy versus laity and who can do what.

I'll take it a step further and challenge our language. When we talk about planting *a* church, there's no such thing. It's *the* church, not *a* church. So when people tell me they feel called to plant a church, I generally say, "I doubt it," you know, just to mess with them a little bit, just to get their attention. Now, if you want to plant *the* church, I'm all over that. If you want to plant *a* church, that typically means you're going out to plant a worship service. And a church grows up around it, and then you have a bunch of consumers again.

Rev. Vasantharaj Albert
Vice-President of the Non-Denominational Association of Interdependent Churches (NAIC)

Most of the indigenous churches are not under any denomination. They are independent and small. Most of the pastors of those churches have only a little training or no training at all. Not even informal training. They just jump into the arena and start leading the church. So, sometimes it looks a little out of control, humanly speaking. But I think the Holy Spirit is leading them.

My observation is that God is going to use house churches, not the denominational churches. Most of the churches will be led by people—we would say lay leaders—who take the responsibility of leading these small churches. And that brings several challenges. Because what I believe is, no church is independent. I mean, one church is born out of the work of the believers from another church. I think in God's Kingdom, every church is connected organically and spiritually. So, how do we best bring a structural expression of that association God has already created among these churches—a structure that would give them complete freedom to respond to the leading of the Holy Spirit without any control from the above? And at the same time, how do we have them come together and work together?

In Acts 20, Paul called together the elders from the city of Ephesus. There were house churches led by a team of elders, but they all came when Paul called them to come together. So though they were independent churches led by elders, Paul somehow connected them with each other—in a kind of hub. Eventually Timothy came and led that hub and gave them direction. But Paul created a kind of structure, a free structure, a hub model that took the gospel out in a concentric way. Paul got them to focus while he enabled them to develop. We can learn from this and do the same.

Dr. J. Watson Selvasingh
Executive Director, Church Growth Association of India; Church Growth Research Center, India

The first prominent challenge that grassroot churches face is the issue of trained leadership, because the majority of pastors are untrained. They have not been to a regular Bible college or seminary. They probably just finished high school, and they may have a certificate or a diploma. But they are zealous for God. Nobody would question that. Unfortunately, their strategy in church planting and also church establishment seems to be very weak. So that's the big challenge—the number one challenge.

The number two challenge is that churches struggle in discipling leaders. The indigenous churches grow in the villages, and probably 60 percent of the population may not be able to read and write. They are from the oral culture, a non-literate background. So to disciple them, you need a different set of skills. Expository preaching will not help. Their culture is different. Their learning methods are different.

We encourage pastors to go back to the early church model of being small, being beautiful. Unfortunately, the concept of megachurches has taken over some of the cities, and these megachurches go around and conduct different seminars. And when these indigenous pastors see or hear that there are 25,000 people in one church, they believe that needs to be their goal. And this distracts them. So we try to keep them focused. We encourage them to have strong small groups in their own churches.

On another note, one of the misplaced priorities is that pastors think that Sunday morning celebrations are crucial. And don't get me wrong, they're important. I'm not saying they're not. But the whole thing operates towards Sunday morning worship. That's it. So is it celebration? Or are we empowering people for discipling? And then it becomes an either/or. And the truth is, you need both. You need to celebrate, and you need to disciple people.

chapter 6

CHANGING LANDSCAPE, RESPONSIVE CHURCH

Chapter 6
Changing Landscape, Responsive Church

Up until 1851, when the telegraph was introduced in a few major cities of India, postal service was the only means of communication throughout the country. Still, this new technology's reach was limited, and most of India remained reliant on postal communication. Then in 1881, Oriental Telephone Company Limited of England opened the first telephone exchanges in four of India's largest cities; and in 1882, the first organized telephone service was made available to ninety-three subscribers. Fast-forward to today. India ranks second in the world for telecommunications subscribers, internet subscriptions, and app downloads. So, in fewer than 150 years, India has gone from a mere ninety-three individuals who used telephones to 1.2 billion telecom subscribers.

This information is staggering, but rapid change is happening on many fronts—and not just in India. No one can deny that today is wildly different from yesterday, and certainly tomorrow will be unrecognizable in ways we can't even imagine. The church, then, while holding fast to the truth, must be agile, flexible, and responsive to change. We need to be grounded in the word, animated by the Spirit, and have our eyes wide open to see where and how God is working. The challenges before us are new, and because of that, the opportunities before us are new as well! It is true around the world and should be considered widely.

It's no coincidence that the model of the church we see in the New Testament has always been well-suited to meet the need of the hour.

The Unleashed Church Is Essential in a Changing Landscape

Today the developing world provides us with extreme examples of rapid change, and therefore my homeland of India is an excellent case study in how an evolving environment requires a nimble, responsive, New Testament-style church. Consider some of the varied shifts impacting the new Indian landscape: technological advances, religious fundamentalism, hypernationalism, climate change, population migration. As people are confronted with modern realities, individuals and entire communities are finding that their perspectives, attitudes, hopes, dreams, and fears have changed. For a moment, let's step inside twenty-first century India and acclimate ourselves to some of its evolving composition.

Technological Advances

All over the world, technology is evolving almost faster than we can keep up. It could not be truer in India! Industries around artificial intelligence, robotics, virtual reality, data analytics, and 3D printing are being woven into India's new economy and are inspiring new products, solutions, and underlying education structures. Much of this technology explosion is a net positive for the Indian people, although the technological landscape represents something like a new territory, one which requires mapping and navigation.

It will be interesting to see how some of the value of new technology plays out. Will the poor and marginalized remain cut off in this new venture, as they have been from so many others, or will they benefit too? Since much of technology today circles around communication, how will India's increasingly authoritarian government use technology to limit certain communication and to propagate other communication?

WhatsApp, owned by Facebook, has its biggest market share in India. This encrypted communication tool has been a safety net for those of us who want to talk about Christian ministry freely. At the same time, as *Digital Trends* reported in August of 2019, "[the] platform has been inundated with an around-the-clock avalanche of misinformation—misleading mobs into lynching innocents and enabling partisans to abuse its far-reaching presence for political gain."

This situation and others emerging from the tech world are certainly a double-edged sword. How can the church take advantage of the communication capabilities that flow from new technology? How can believers share the gospel in ways that are less likely to be restricted?

Religious Fundamentalism and Hyper-nationalism

In May 2019, India witnessed the unprecedented landslide victory of a single large political party, the Bharatiya Janata Party (BJP). This party campaigned on the platform of converting the world's largest democracy into a Hindu nation united by one religion, one culture, and one language. In the process, traditionally held views of democracy, nationalism, and patriotism are being redefined. In this emerging context, to be anything other than a Hindu is to deny being an Indian!

The "saffron" BJP party, so called because the color is considered holy in India, now stands on its own without having to lean on the crutches of coalitions or alliances to govern the nation. There may be some value to their scope of power, considering the way India has been fragmented and divided. Nevertheless, considering the track record of this political party, all I can say is that we have moved into perilous times. This is not a sudden change in direction but is a move of increasing intensity. Hindu right-wing militant outfits such as the Rashtriya Swayamsevak Sangh (RSS) and Vishva Hindu Parishad (VHP) are now empowered to forcefully implement their objectives. Their agenda is no longer hidden; it is out in the open. What is it? To create a Hindu India.

Needless to say, these political developments have deep implications for the church in India and Christian ministries, not only in India but in the entire region of South Asia. This present trend will definitively determine the course of Christian missions in this region. We are so grateful that God is building a nimble, indigenous church in the villages of India. We are not afraid of persecution, and we are glad that our churches are not deliberately dressing themselves in Western trappings and needlessly calling attention to themselves. Churches that introduce Jesus culture (but not Western culture) will still stand out, and yes, even offend, but not because of Western cultural trappings.

Water Crisis

Another factor in India's evolving composition is the water crisis. Complex and acute, the crisis is already a forceful driver of human activity as well as a looming threat to many in a fragile geo-economic environment. According to the *MIT Technology Review,* "More than 600 million Indians face acute water shortages. Seventy percent of the nation's water supply is contaminated, causing an estimated 200,000 deaths a year. Some twenty-one cities could run out of groundwater as early as next year, including Bangalore and New Delhi. 40 percent of the population, or more than 500 million people, will have 'no access to drinking water' by 2030." At this very moment, while I am writing this book, Chennai is on the front page of major American newspapers. This city of 9.1 million people has actually run completely out of water. The crisis is unfolding.

As India Gospel League's barefoot pastors head out into villages, leading with the gospel and planting churches, they establish thriving, Christ-centered communities that overflow with love. One way that we seek to demonstrate the generous, overflowing love of God is by helping our local churches provide clean water in their villages. Many rural villages do not have "at least basic water," meaning women must make multiple trips each day to find water for drinking, cooking, and hygiene. The need for clean water is so obvious and so great that it is often a primary concern for our local pastors.

Once a church is established in a village, the pastor is able to apply to IGL to have a well drilled in their community. Each application is reviewed in our IGL India offices and is evaluated based on the relative need of that village. When an application is approved, the pastor then works with local officials to coordinate zoning applications, permits, etc. Not unlike construction work everywhere, this part can take a painfully long time—typically six to twelve weeks.

When documentation is finally complete, IGL releases funding, and the pastor hires local companies to drill the well. Once finished, the well is officially opened to the community during a ribbon-cutting ceremony. A representative from IGL joins the church and villagers for a wonderfully exciting day that typically includes a Bible teaching, singing, treats, and, of course, collecting clean, fresh water! These wells are almost always drilled near the church and are available for the use of anyone in the village. What a gift! And what an opportunity to share the Good News!

Because of the "boots on the ground" infrastructure of IGL in India and the relationships built with barefoot pastors and their communities, Western believers have a direct line to give the gift of clean water to parched villages. It's truly amazing how much "bang for your buck" you get when you give in India; and donating an IGL well is an exceptional value. Each well costs $1,250 from start to finish. This small amount is something a family, a small group, a Sunday school class, or a group of friends could go in on together. What a privilege for God's children to be able to share his resources in such a practical and refreshing way!

Just this past year, IGL, with the help of its partners, was able to provide nearly eighty water wells to villages that had no reasonable access to clean water. As supply of this basic human need for clean water continues to dwindle, it would be magnificent to see the church step in to be "living water" in India.

Climate Change

Sea level changes, the rise in average temperature, and extreme swings between drought and heavy monsoon seasons are all part of the groanings of climate change. This increasingly rapid evolution will have significant impact, again, on the most vulnerable. Aayushi Awasthi, a writer for the BBC, said in the article "Why India Needs to Worry About Climate Change," "[Climate change will] disproportionately affect disadvantaged and vulnerable populations through food insecurity, higher food prices, income losses, lost livelihood opportunities, adverse health impacts, and population displacements." India stands to be one of the nations most affected, given its huge population and levels of inequality and poverty. The church will be affected too, but more importantly, how will it respond?

I am reminded of the witness of the early church in the Roman Empire. When two great waves of plagues battered the city of Rome, tens of thousands of people were killed in the gruesome, widespread pandemics. The wealthy and able fled the cities, hoping to survive outside the crowded and dirty city centers. But the Christians? They stayed. There are records of this time, written both by pagan and Christian leaders, which note the Christian response. Eusebius, who was the bishop of Caesarea in 341 AD, recorded that during the plague, "All day long some of [the Christians] tended to the dying and to their burial, countless numbers with no one to care for them. Others gathered together from all parts of the city a multitude of those withered from famine and distributed bread to them all."

After Eusebius' death, Emperor Julian wrote a letter to a pagan priest, complaining that the "impious Galileans" were caring for the sick and dying to such an extent that it highlighted the government's own inaction. He suggested that the pagan (and government affiliated) priests copy what the Christians were doing. Unsurprisingly, this was not very effective. The reason? The call to die to one's self for the sake of another is unsustainable without the love and power of a real, eternal God.

Pray with me that the unleashed church will overflow with the same kind of love and practical concern in the face of India's deadly drought today as the Christians did in Rome so long ago. And may Jesus' name be made known because of it.

Population Migration

Another aspect of India's evolving composition—and the final one I'd like to mention here—is population migration. India's 2011 Census reported that a stunning 165 million people moved around throughout the country in inter- and intra-state migration. It's no surprise that migration movements have always been a significant factor in the spread of ideas and religion. Of course, people migrate for a host of reasons: to seek economic stability or religious freedom, to escape natural disasters or famine are just a few. In the New Testament, we read that when people were persecuted, they were scattered; as a result, everywhere they went, people came to the Lord and churches were planted! Because migrations are movements of people, and people carry the gospel message, migrations have always been important, organic pathways for sharing the Good News.

My friend Jim Lyon calls this migration "riding the rails of the gospel." A few months ago, he was telling me about a church he works with in downtown Seattle. The leadership was discouraged and felt that they couldn't make much impact in the vastly changing environment that had grown up around their urban fellowship. "From a window in the church," Jim told me, "I could see fourteen brand new skyscrapers that belonged to Amazon alone. That's about 45,000 people in those fourteen buildings, all twenty- and thirty-somethings.

"Imagine them finding Jesus," he said. "If they do, they'll ride the rails of the gospel all across the world."

This is true in the States, and it is certainly true in India today! We will be wise to consider the opportunities presented by migration. Our high investment/low control model of discipleship is an amazing preparation for ministry that is on the move.

The Third Wave, Unleashed Church Is Both Unchanging *and* Flexible

God is not surprised by the changing composition of India. In fact, he has prepared his people—his church—for such a time as this. The Third Wave, unleashed, church-planting model is primed to step into the opportunities of a shifting landscape. It is effective because while the core message is precious and unchanging, the means and methods are flexible and free, with a high value on growing gospel seeds in indigenous soil. Cornelis Bennema and Paul Joshua Bhakiaraj, coauthors of *Indian and Christian: Changing Identities in Modern India*, have distilled what they call "the characteristics of Indian Christian identity." While this description can and should apply to all people and cultures, it is interesting to drill down into how it plays out in Third Wave ministry in India today.

- The Christian identity is a religious identity, not attached to any particular geopolitical entity, ethnicity, or culture.
- This identity is inclusive and transformational, one that transcends and absorbs rather than abrogates existing

identities.

- The Christian identity is one that unites and directs other identities toward Christ.

Of course, scripture is the foundation and springboard for such a relationship with the gospel. Several narratives come to mind that describe the principle of the "unchanging and flexible" gospel. First, think of Jesus and the Samaritan woman at the well. Jesus broke all kinds of cultural norms in order to share himself with this outcast woman. He not only entered into her unique culture (that of a woman at the margins of her community), but he transcended it with himself: the Messiah, to be worshiped in spirit and in truth.

Remember too Peter and the vision of "pigs in a blanket" from Acts chapter 10. This astounding series of events stopped Peter in his tracks and cleared the way for the gospel to be shared with Gentiles who feared and hungered for God.

And when Jesus meets the Roman centurion in Matthew 8, he cites the man's faith. Actually, he does more than that. He celebrates the man's faith, calling it greater than what he has seen in all of Israel! It is faith in Christ that is central, not the man's background, ethnicity, trappings, position, or culture.

Paul concisely and concretely lays out the principle of "unchanging and flexible" in 1 Corinthians 9:19–23.

> For though I am free from all, I have made myself a servant to all, that I might win more of them. To the Jews I became as a Jew, in order to win Jews. To those under the law I became as one under the law (though not being myself under the law) that I might win those under the law. To those outside the law I became as one outside the law (not being outside the law of God but under the law of Christ) that I might win those outside the law. To the weak I became weak, that I might win the weak. I have become all things to all people, that by all means I might save some. I do it all for the sake of the gospel, that I may share with them in its blessings. (ESV)

The result of these wide-open doors for the gospel is that in the end, the Kingdom of God will be filled—is *destined* to be filled as promised in the book of Revelation—with people from every tribe and nation who have fallen at the feet of Jesus. Praise the Lord.

> After this I looked, and behold, a great multitude that no one could number, from every nation, from all tribes and peoples and languages, standing before the throne and before the Lamb, clothed in white robes, with palm branches in their hands, and crying out with a loud voice, "Salvation belongs to our God who sits on the throne, and to the Lamb!" (Revelation 7:9–10 ESV)

In light of this great promise, however, we must not forget that there is still much work to be done. Embedded in all the motion and change in our world today are the needs of real individuals. Frankly, those whom we consider "the least of these" are usually the most affected by this shifting landscape. Herein is the opportunity for the church! In India, we are seeing the church shine a bright light through an "other focused" passion for the Great Commission. We are witnessing the indigenous (and often impoverished) body of Christ love and serve the lost and even more needy.

In the next chapter, we'll take a closer look at some examples of God's people "giving out of need," and we'll explore how such a spirit of open-handed generosity builds stable and lively communities.

REFLECT

1. I mentioned the witness of second-century Christians in the Roman Empire. They certainly did not think that their efforts would rid Rome of the plague. Why do you think they stayed?

2. What opportunities do you see in the changing landscape around you? How could "unchanging and flexible" in your own life help you to meet these opportunities? What are ways your

church could respond to these opportunities?

3. Have you seen the Western church struggle with being *both* "changing" *and* "inflexible," thus distorting the core message of the Bible while holding tight to man-made tradition? What are examples? How could this be counteracted? What can you or your church do to help?

CHALLENGE

1. *The Lord is my rock, my fortress and my deliverer; my God is my rock, in whom I take refuge, my shield and the horn of my salvation, my stronghold. (Psalm 18:2 NIV)*

    Every good and perfect gift is from above, coming down from the Father of the heavenly lights, who does not change like shifting shadows. (James 1:17 NIV)

    Jesus Christ is the same yesterday and today and forever. (Hebrews 13:8 NIV)

    The Lord is not slow in keeping his promise, as some understand slowness. Instead he is patient with you, not wanting anyone to perish, but everyone to come to repentance. (Peter 3:9 NIV)

    Many scripture passages describe God's unchanging nature. Meditate on how that nature is revealed in each of these passages for a few moments.

2. How does knowing that the Lord does not change in character or intention affect the way that you experience change around you?

3. God seems to do unexpected things often in the narratives of scripture. He does and allows unexpected things in our lives

today! List some of the things about God that do not change, even though our circumstances do. Do you think that God is unchanging and flexible? Why or why not?

KINGDOM VOICES

Rev. Vasantharaj Albert
Vice-President of the Non-Denominational Association of
Interdependent Churches (NAIC)

One of the driving forces for our ministry comes out of Matthew 28:19–20: Go make disciples of all people groups, baptizing them, teaching them what Jesus Christ has commanded us to. And the [traditional] church in India has had a particular failure in making disciples. Most of the churches are in celebration mode, not discipling mode. Often the big churches are a model for other churches, so that is going on even in indigenous missions and a number of missions in India. They also do not place much importance on discipling the believers.

I don't think we can make disciples without small group dynamics. Sunday worship is necessary. That's a biblical model we have to practice. But in addition to that, we encourage people to form small Bible study groups and meet maybe once or twice in a week. And we use Bible storytelling, so we teach them how to tell Bible stories. We want people to interact, not just listen to someone who has prepared the message and delivered it to them. Asking the right questions is the most important part of our storytelling.

You don't see results immediately, maybe not for one or two years. But if you are consistently doing that, you will definitely see results. And part of that discipling is they have to go and plant churches. They have to go and share the story that they heard that week and pray for the person they shared it with. And we help them to see the importance of the spiritual practice of prayer. I can't say yet that it's successful, but now pastors are realizing that it should be done.

chapter 7

GROWTH COMES FROM GIVING

UNLEASHED

Chapter 7
Growth Comes from Giving

In late August 2008, angry mobs swarmed the forests and villages of Kandhamal, destroying homes, burning churches, and hunting Christians. Abu Salam, his wife, and his two little children had moved to a tiny village in Kandhamal from another part of Odisha several years earlier to share the Good News of Jesus Christ. When the riots broke out, Abu, his family, and a group of brothers and sisters gathered in their tiny church building to pray. The four walls were not a protection for them. Enraged rioters burst into the church and immediately set it on fire. Terrified and disoriented, the families inside pressed to the doorways and fled into the surrounding forest.

They would not learn until later that thousands of homes belonging to Christians in the region had been burned, close to one hundred churches were destroyed, and scores of brothers and sisters were brutally tortured and murdered. There were thousands of people in the vast forested area of the Kandhamal region, hiding, trying to survive.

Abu Salam, his wife and his children were among the families who had run to the forest for shelter, but in the chaos they became separated from one another. Abu lived in the forest for four months with no change of clothes, surviving on roots and leaves. He had no idea where his family was. His wife was alone in the forest, desperately searching for her husband and children, who had vanished into the trees.

Four months went by, and eventually Abu got word that it was safe to come out. He heard that many survivors had gathered near the edge of the forest. Unbelievably, there Abu was reunited with his wife and children. They were together, bereft and traumatized, but safe.

Once reunited, they spared no time in returning to the little village, Nuisia, where they'd been living. Abu Salam and his wife felt that God was calling them to re-gather the congregation that had been together in Nuisia. They rebuilt their tiny church building. But the militants returned and burned it down again.

At this time, India Gospel League came to the Kandhamal area, looking for ways to support and aid the thousands of refugees and homeless believers who were slowly returning from the forests. I met Abu Salam and his family, and he told me about his passion to continue to preach the gospel in this hostile place. IGL spread the word to our allies in the West, and several American churches began to gather funds to build a Life Center in Nuisia. Indigenous churches in Tamil Nadu came together and raised 150,000 rupees to contribute to the Nuisia church and Life Center.

Several years ago as I was talking to Abu Salom, he told me the most remarkable thing. "God called me to this place and to these people," he said. "Considering how God is blessing us today—a church of 145 believers, a nice church building where we can worship God together—all of that suffering seems insignificant, and I would do it again."

Life in God's Economy

God's economy says that tending to the flourishing of others *contributes* to rather than diminishes our own flourishing; yet day in and day out, we are surrounded by cultural values that contrast wildly with this Kingdom value. Human wisdom says, "Get all you can and keep it." The church is in great danger of adopting this idea and giving it a "churchy twist." Believers can come to believe that personal stability and spiritual growth come from high investment in themselves, in their own families, and in their own "backyards." Eventually, though, under this worldly wisdom, the lifeblood of individuals, family, and community dries up. God did not design us as holding tanks. We are conduits, made to drink deeply from living waters and to share the overflow with other thirsty souls.

The Bible clearly teaches that growth comes from giving—and even from dying to ourselves. Vibrancy and vitality thrive in the soil of generosity. I've witnessed this phenomenon so broadly in our work that I'd like to take a deep dive and dedicate an entire chapter to it.

We'll start in the scripture and then look at how this lifestyle of giving unfolds today.

You've Got to Die

Nothing could be more clear nor more jarring than what Jesus says in John 12:24: "Truly, truly, I say to you, unless a grain of wheat falls into the earth and dies, it remains alone; but if it dies, it bears much fruit" (ESV). Let these words never become a Christian platitude, something with which we feel overly familiar and friendly. No one should be able to read this with glazed eyes and a gentle nod. Jesus, the one to whom we have entrusted ourselves, is calling us to follow him into death. And this is not a sanitized version of death. The pregnant seed, the one that will multiply and grow into a great harvest, must first be buried in dark, dank soil. Underground, the pressures of its environment will conspire over time to soften, erode, and rot the seed coat. Finally, it will crack, and the new life of a fruitful plant springs out toward sunshine.

This is the pattern Jesus taught, and it is the pattern to which he called his disciples. Primarily, it is the pattern that he lived out—our fruitful forerunner, bursting out of death into abundant life.

Giving Out of Need—The Macedonian Church

In 2 Corinthians, Paul wrote to the church in Corinth:

> And now, brothers, we want you to know about the grace that God has given the Macedonian churches. In the midst of a very severe trial, their overflowing joy and their extreme poverty welled up in rich generosity. For I testify that they gave as much as they were able, and even beyond their ability. Entirely on their own, they urgently pleaded with us for the privilege of sharing in this service to the Lord's people. And they exceeded our expectations: They gave themselves first of all to the Lord, and then by the will of God also to us. (8:1–5 NIV)

Paul had been asking the churches he'd planted to contribute to the needs of the church in Jerusalem. The believers there were systematically losing almost everything when they converted, and they were in dire straits. In the passage above, Paul appeals to the Corinthian church, which apparently was less than motivated to give at the time. To make the appeal, he cites the generosity of the Macedonian church. The Macedonian church was not one single church community but the churches we know at Philippi and Thessalonica. While these cities, especially Philippi, were relatively prosperous, it seems that the converts in those churches came from the lower classes. Many would have been unable to find work because of discrimination and persecution.

Let's go through Paul's own words and mine them for distinctives of generous, flourishing community.

- **God-given grace**: Paul is quick to note that the generosity and overflowing nature of the Macedonian churches has its source in God's generosity. He recognized it, and we can assume that the community did too. Their loose handedness has all the marks of people who are ultimately secure and see themselves as conduits of a supply that is fresh every day.

- **Veterans of severe trial:** What happens to people who walk through significant trials? Generally, one of three things: 1) They are crushed by the trial and become bitter and self-protective. 2) They make it through the trial and credit themselves, becoming proud and self-focused. 3) As in the case of the Macedonian churches, they are afflicted in every way but not crushed. Rather, through the trial, they find salvation and hope and even joy at the generous and sustaining hand of the Father. Finding the Father to be so faithful a provider in trials frees one up to give generously, whether in want or in plenty.

- **A combination of joy and poverty leads to rich giving:** This distinctive is a bit mysterious and certainly falls under the umbrella of "the backward wisdom of God." This equation (joy + poverty = generosity) doesn't make much sense if we evaluate it with worldly wisdom. The Bible is full of stories of the rich who have come to trust in their riches. Think of how John characterizes the Laodicean church: "I am rich. I don't need a thing!" (Revelation 3:17 NLT). How can a community that "doesn't need a thing" enter into the gospel relationship that God offers, in which he is always the giver and we are always dependent receivers?

If being poor creates a straighter path to recognizing our need (as in Matthew 5), then it creates fertile ground for finding supply at the generous hand of God. A deep, experiential recognition of God's generous supply absolutely results in joy and the freedom to steward rather than hoard his goodness.

- **Generous beyond their ability:** When a community is convinced that God is in the business of giving and they are persuaded that he is a provider and sustainer, they will not evaluate their ability to give based on the number in their own bank accounts or the coins in their own pockets. Trusting in him who owns the cattle on a thousand hills, they are freed up to radically—and even foolishly—give. Why are we so afraid of looking a fool anyways? David, full of joy at a chance to serve the Lord, said, "Yes, and I am willing to look even more foolish than this . . ." (2 Samuel 6:22 NLT).

God loves a cheerful giver because a cheerful giver is dancing in step with the heart of God. This storyline was not a hypothetical one for the Macedonian church. They really were impoverished. They really were marginalized. Giving "foolishly" would be a real-life sacrifice that played out in how much food they ate. Yet, they gave.

- **Counted it a privilege to serve the saints:** God was doing something of incredible, historic importance in the first century. Wouldn't any of us be grateful to have just a pinch of that experience? Of course, we know it would be an utmost privilege to participate in a movement that changed the world. We know that now, and the Macedonian church knew it *then*. They wanted to be part of what God was doing! Giving to that end was no obligation, nor chore, nor duty, nor measured tithe. It was a joy! And more than a joy—a *privilege*! The scripture says they urgently plead for this privilege. They understood that the opportunity to be part of something so much bigger than themselves was only more grace.

- **Gave themselves first to the Lord:** In many ways, these Macedonian Christians were living the dream. They were riding on the wind of the Holy Spirit, responsive to his direction, fruitful, and significant. (Aren't we still talking about them today?) It seems that as a whole, their ethos had become that they were the Lord's. That they would be living sacrifices. That their spiritual service of worship would be to give all of themselves to him. Along with Paul, they could say, "I know whom I have believed, and am persuaded that he is able to keep that which I have committed unto him against that day" (2 Timothy 1:12 KJV).

Losing Our Lives, Gaining Joy—God's Supply Chain

I want to follow this look at the Macedonian church with a few telling comments Paul makes in his letter to the Philippians. In chapter 2, Paul says, "But I will rejoice even if I lose my life, pouring it out like a liquid offering to God, just like your faithful service is an offering to God. And I want all of you to share that joy. Yes, you should rejoice, and I will share your joy" (Philippians 2:17–18 NLT). Paul had planted this church and was leading it down the pathway of God's backward wisdom: "*I* have poured my life out, *you* are pouring your life out, and we are all going to experience so much joy together as a result." A community that gives itself to the flourishing of others will flourish.

In chapter 4, Paul reflects on the generosity of this "least of these" church and again describes God's supply chain at work:

> Moreover, as you Philippians know, in the early days of your acquaintance with the gospel, when I set out from Macedonia, not one church shared with me in the matter of

giving and receiving, except you only; for even when I was in Thessalonica, you sent me aid more than once when I was in need. Not that I desire your gifts; what I desire is that more be credited to your account. I have received full payment and have more than enough. I am amply supplied, now that I have received from Epaphroditus the gifts you sent. They are a fragrant offering, an acceptable sacrifice, pleasing to God. And my God will meet all your needs according to the riches of his glory in Christ Jesus. (Philippians 4:15–19 NIV)

Just as Paul says, when we give, more will be credited to our account. God will meet our needs from his storehouse of riches. We can be amply supplied. We get to please God. The poured-out life is a life of abundance, overflow, relationship, significance, and joy! Praise the Lord for his great generosity!

Full Baskets

Perhaps the supply chain of flourishing is most succinctly summed up after the feeding of the five thousand. Matthew writes, "They all ate and were satisfied, and the disciples picked up twelve basketfuls of broken pieces that were left over" (Matthew 18:20 NIV). In her book, *The Broken Way*, Ann Voskamp sums it up like this: "The bread that we give to feed another's soul is what miraculously feeds ours." This truth is not an idea or a suggestion that pops up here and there in scripture. No, it is how the Kingdom operates. It's woven into God's story everywhere. All you need to do is look.

If the feeding of the five thousand gives us the most succinct look, Jesus' own story is the most profound. Who God is—his power, his glory, his tremendous love—is perfectly revealed in Jesus giving up his privilege to live and die in an act of love for enemies. For the joy set before him, he endured the cross. While we likely feel mildly uncomfortable with "foolish" giving, this radical inversion of our human view of power and glory sets us on edge. We can't easily make sense of it. And perhaps we don't want to. There is no more significant critique of our world's value systems.

Jesus is our example, to be sure, and he is also our power source for sacrificial love. It is a beautiful thing to see the joy of knowing Jesus poured out in generosity even today. Let's take a look at how that generosity is unfolding in India and then all the way across the globe in a small corner of Ohio.

Stories: Gaining Joy through Giving

Andie and the Women with a Mission

Andie is a quiet, observant young woman who headed up our travel department in the North American office in Ohio for several years before she had children. Andie leans more toward hesitation than haste; is convicted yet struggles with fear; and has a huge heart but is constrained by ongoing health issues. I asked her to share her story because it not only captures the explosive growth that the Lord worked in her heart and spiritual stature, but it also illustrates the fountain of joy bubbling up from significant saints in India. This is what Andie told me:

> In 2012, I had the privilege to attend and teach at an IGL Women with a Mission Conference in India. At the time, I was an India Gospel League employee and was sent to India to get a firsthand view of the mission I supported from the US. I'm so grateful to have had this opportunity. This trip changed my life and my perspective on the world forever. The funny thing is, I didn't want to go! I was happy and comfortable here in the United States. I could sit in my air-conditioned office and send emails or tell the amazing stories of people in India doing miraculous things for the Lord, but I didn't feel the need to go see for myself. I'd heard about it, and that was good enough! I had a lot of excuses—from poor health to funding the trip— but, in reality, I was fearful and selfish.
>
> There are many stories and experiences from my trip to India that I will never forget and that changed me forever. God took me far out of my comfort zone and showed me firsthand that you don't have to say the "right thing" or live in the "right place" to be effective for Christ. One of the most touching experiences of that trip happened while we were teaching at

a national women's conference. These annual conferences are attended by women who lead in their local churches. Hundreds of women from all over India attend. Some women travel for days to get there, sleeping in fields or wherever they can along the way. Everyone comes to hear Bible teachings and to get equipped so they can go back home and equip the women they lead.

For many of the women, the journey to get to these conferences is long and hard. We take for granted how freely we can open a book, read the Bible, listen to a podcast, or drive to church to learn about Jesus. Yet they don't have that kind of access to biblical teachings. So, to them, a long hard journey to hear about Christ can't be passed up.

Participants praying at a Women with a Mission Meeting

There were about seven hundred women in attendance at one of the conferences where we were teaching. On the last day, volunteers were passing around white plastic buckets, and I noticed the women dropping envelopes and bills into them. I asked one of the workers what they were doing, and she said that they were collecting money to send out barefoot pastors. These men were being sent out by their home churches, but their churches were too poor to give them any financial help. I had to stop and think about that for a moment. I asked again, "What are these women collecting money for?" She explained that they collected money from their own local churches to help support new barefoot pastors. By the time I was at that conference in 2012, the more established IGL churches had collectively given enough money to send over 120 barefoot pastors out to evangelize those who've never heard the name of Christ.

I was blown away. Here I was in a room full of women who lived in a society that is oppressive to women. They were the poorest of the poor. And they were happily giving money to support the spread of the gospel. They were excited. They were grateful to hear how many pastors were being supported. They wanted to help. As a selfish, comfort-seeking American, I could not imagine living in poverty and then willingly parting with my money.

But these women knew it was worth it. They had come to know Christ as their Lord and savior. They learned that they are loved by the Creator. They had been told for the first time ever that salvation is for them too. That the God of the universe loves them and has a plan for them. Even as untouchables. Even as women living in an oppressive society. So if they could give away what little they had so that someone else could hear that message, it was worth it. As I sat there taking all this in, Galatians 3:28 came to mind, "There is neither Jew nor Gentile, neither slave nor free, nor is there male and female, for you are all one in Christ Jesus" (NIV).

Pastor Benjamin

In 1989, a teenager named Benjamin was walking down a dirt road in his hometown of Mettur when he happened to notice a colorful scrap of paper under his feet. Certainly, there were other scraps of paper on the ground, and certainly a seventeen-year-old boy might have had his mind on other things. On this day, Benjamin noticed the paper and stooped to pick it up off the bustling dirt road. It seemed to be a ripped advertisement, but he could make out these words: "Think about your life." Benjamin was a young man on the cusp of adulthood who had come to Christ after a miraculous healing from illness. Uniquely, his family had also come to Christ and were spiritually rich; yet like so many others in Mettur, they were materially impoverished. Indeed, at this time of his life, Benjamin had a lot to think about—his future and how he could help care for his family. He was, in fact, thinking about his life!

Upon closer inspection, Benjamin noticed that the paper said something about God, and it listed an address in Salem for "Samuel Stephens" at an organization called IGL. Perhaps seventeen-year-old boys are naturally curious and prone to adventure, and certainly God uses these qualities to steer and direct them. That night, Benjamin was still thinking about this little scrap of paper, and so he got out pen and paper and wrote me a letter. He inquired about IGL and wondered how our ministry might connect with his own direction in life.

When I received his letter, I invited Benjamin to come visit me. He made the fifty-kilometer journey from his industrial city to Salem, where my family and I were spending our early days on the Sharon Campus. When Benjamin arrived, he told me the whole story of finding the paper on the road, about his family, and about his conversion. I welcomed Benjamin as a brother in Christ, but he seemed taken aback by the camaraderie, almost as if he didn't expect such a warm welcome.

The Lord allowed me to see something unique in Benjamin: his youth, his zeal, his inquisitive nature. I took note that the Lord seemed to be moving in this young man's life, and I wanted to be a part of it. Although I wanted Benjamin to come to Sharon to be trained in the word, he obviously had a responsibility to his family in Mettur. I was able to share a sum of money with him, and I encouraged him to go back home to take care of his family. Then we prayed that when the time was right, he could come back to Sharon to study and apprentice as a pastor.

Today, Benjamin has been a pastor for thirty-one years. He has suffered beatings, rejection, long spells of seemingly fruitless toil, and having his church building burned down. But he has become a pillar of strength, a spring of generosity, and a fruitful servant in his community. He remains adventurous and bold—his greatest desire is to serve where others are wary to go. In a recent conversation, Pastor Benjamin was asked about his needs. His reply is instructive to us. First, he responded that God has already blessed him with everything that he needs. That said, there are ongoing needs that he is presenting to the Lord: protection for the church, as there is active violence toward his congregation; a restroom for the people at the church to use; and clean drinking water for his village and church community.

Notably, he also mentioned that his village church takes a financial collection at their meetings. The funds gathered by this community, which is persecuted and is without clean water or plumbing, are used as a missionary offering, a contribution to those who are traveling to reach unreached places, and for a specific pastor who is reaching the unreached in another village. In addition, the youth are commissioned to take provisions collected by the church out to their community, offering food and clothing to those in greater poverty than they are. As they visit widows and other desperately poor people, they share the word of God with hopes of bringing many into God's Kingdom. Pastor Benjamin says of his village church, "The more we give, the more God blesses us."

In this same conversation, Pastor Benjamin said something that really resonated with me and beautifully expresses the principle that "growth comes from giving." He said:

> In this world, we have not brought anything in, and we will not take anything out. God has blessed us with just one life, and it should be a peaceful life. But peace won't come through investing in the things of the world. It comes when we invest

in the Kingdom of God. When we give back to the poor and to families who are broken down and who have no peace themselves. When we help to educate children, and when we buy land for those who have no homes. When we invest in the Kingdom first, we link peace with our own homes. I believe that God blesses us and opens the floodgates of heaven when we start giving back to God. Our hands are open to give.

Freedom Fellowship

Freedom Fellowship is a mid-sized church in Northeast Ohio. This fellowship does not have a building or a physical address. They use facilities at a nearby university campus during the school year and enjoy meeting in parks during the summer. This is a young, energetic church in which over 70 percent of the people are under thirty years old. During the week, the majority of their 390 members spend time in small, home group Bible studies, in even smaller "cell group" Bible studies, and many also meet for discipleship as well.

Over the past ten years or so, this group has steadily become more and more invested in the work of India Gospel League. We have faithful and generous supporters from all across the United States, Canada, and Australia, but I want to share about this church in particular because, to most people, it might not seem well-positioned for generosity. After all, most of its members are students living off of cheap pizzas and doing odd jobs to pay rent. Yet this young congregation is giving in remarkable ways.

Erin

Several years ago, Erin, a vibrant young college student and member of Freedom Fellowship, was reading *You and Me Forever* by Frances and Lisa Chan. Erin said of the book, "They talk about Jesus and getting close to Jesus by getting out on the battlefield. I thought, I want to be close to Jesus, and I want to be close to where Jesus is working." Jesus is definitely working in Erin's college ministry. In fewer than ten years, it has grown from a tiny group of eight students to a collection of eight home churches, each bursting at the seams! Even so, Jesus was about to lead Erin into even more significance.

Erin with pictures and letters from Sopitha

After a few of Erin's friends had gone to India to teach at a Women With a Mission Conference, and she began to grow a desire to participate in the Spirit's work in India. "I wanted to be a part of this," she said. "And I realized I could do what I can from Ohio, even though I don't have feet on the ground in India." When Erin heard about IGL's "Love One More" initiative (a ministry supporting India's children in a variety of ways), she decided to take on that commitment. Here's what she had to say about coming to that decision:

> I had just a little bit of hesitation about committing, but in the end, it came down to willingness. There was a time when I had a perspective about my income that was more like, "Hey, this is mine!" But the Lord started teaching me that there's another perspective, which is that none of this is mine. It's actually all the Lord's. The only question is what I am going to do with what he gave me. Am I going to be generous and celebrate how he's given me things that I can give away, or am I going to sit on it and keep it for myself? After a short time of considering "Love One More," I decided, yeah, I'm going to do what I can with what the Lord has given me.

Since then, Erin has sponsored two children, contributed to an Adopt a Village project, and helped provide a motorcycle for the pastor in that village. She's already made plans to support another child in the near future! Not only is she growing in generosity, but this generosity has energized her own spiritual life and ministry. She says:

> My perspective has opened up. Everything is not about the here and now, or my little corner of the world. God's mission is happening everywhere, but we can get so stuck sometimes just focusing on our ministries and what we want. I think it is really awesome to have God's mission broadened in my brain! I get to see evidence of the Holy Spirit and evidence that God exists because of what is happening across the world.

Erin's heart was truly changed. She had a new perspective on how she could use what she had to give to others. She went on to say:

> No matter what you have, you can be a giver! You can pray and tell the Lord you want to give, and he will definitely honor that. The question is, are you going to trust the Lord and count on his nourishment and protection? He will provide more than you ever expected. He can do anything with the little tiny bit you have. So I would strongly recommend trying to be generous! You will overflow with joy and fruit!

The young church that Erin is part of has ministry and world missions on their minds, but it seems that God's work in India has captured them in a unique way. To date, a dozen groups from Freedom Fellowship have traveled to India for teaching trips—that's 12 percent of the church! They have rallied to adopt two villages over the past five years, and they are eager to complete their pledges ahead of time in order to adopt yet another village and see the gospel saturate rural areas. In this one church alone, 124 people sponsor children through "Love One More," and eleven people are supporting barefoot pastors.

Neil

Neil, a thirty-something elder at Freedom Fellowship, took an Eyewitness Trip with IGL in 2013. Four friends, all of whom came to Christ along with Neil during high school, joined him. Neil said, "I remember being in the back of a traveler van in India, sans seatbelt, driving around on crazy roads and writing down numbers on the back of an envelope." The cost to adopt a village was $75,000 over the course of five years. "We realized, yeah, we can totally do this! Forty people would need to be willing to give $32 a month. I was sure we could find forty people in our church of a couple hundred who would be willing to give! We came back, pitched it to the church, and exceeded what we'd hoped to pledge."

To say the church is excited to participate in God's work in India is an understatement. Driven by its young population, they have hosted events like "Basketball for Bibles," a fundraiser to purchase Bibles for IGL, and "Punjab Prom," which raised money for teams to speak at conferences. Year round, apartments and homes are decorated with colorful pictures of children sponsored through "Love One More." Many meet to pray each month for IGL ministry and other gospel work around the globe.

Neil tells me that the effects of Freedom Fellowship joining in with what God is doing in India have been incredible.

> We've had more than a dozen teams visit India to speak at conferences. And this is really smart on IGL's part. Instead

of having people go who are focused on "Oh, I don't like to travel" or "Oh, I don't like spicy food," their focus has to be on giving, not on themselves. They've been asked to prepare, to step outside of their comfort zones, and to get focused totally on other people—on giving. There has been a huge ripple effect: giving even fifty bucks has changed lives! For each one of those individuals who goes to India, I know they come back changed. You can't go to India and not come back changed. You have a kind of awakening. You really see how the other half of the world lives and realize, "I had no idea." It leaves an indelible mark on your heart that you'll never forget.

Neil (center) and friends from his most recent pastor's conference trip, 2017

If you're thinking through how you might begin a story of excitement and participation like this one, Neil suggests that leaders simply create an opportunity: "Present the idea of rallying around India Gospel League to your church. If individuals are moved by the Spirit, how could anything get in the way of that? How could it be stopped? Let the Spirit do his work."

The Four Pillars of India Gospel League

At IGL, our mission is 100 percent about giving away what our generous Father has given us. We describe this mission as standing on four key pillars, each a robust, self-sustaining platform for stewarding our resources.

4 Pillars
OF INDIA GOSPEL LEAGUE MINISTRY

Evangelism & Church Planting
SHARING JESUS WITH UNREACHED VILLAGES

Love One More
LOVING CHILDREN IN NEED

Medical Outreach
CARING FOR THE SICK

Economic Development
CARING FOR THE POOREST OF THE POOR

Evangelism & Church Planting

Sharing Jesus with Unreached Villages

By identifying and training indigenous church planters, IGL reaches villages that have never had a Christian presence. Pastors are encouraged to reach one new village each year. This encourages them to train up new leaders and keep a strong evangelistic focus in their churches.

Medical Outreach

Caring for the Sick

The dramatic poverty experienced by the rural poor means that medical care is scarce or non-existent. IGL works with village church leaders to facilitate basic medical checkups, health clinics, prescription drugs, and through our hospital in Tamil Nadu, even advanced cancer treatments and surgical care. For most villagers, these services are out of reach economically and geographically.

Love One More

Loving Children in Need

The church work we do quickly uncovers practical needs in the village, and children often top the list. Many little ones have been orphaned or face malnourishment and lack of education because their parents are impoverished. Local pastors assess the best ways to serve the children, from Children's Gospel Clubs, to discipleship, to full sponsorship: providing kids in need with food, education, and familial love.

Economic Development

Caring for the Poorest of the Poor

After planting a church in a village, we work with the local pastor to address physical and economic needs in his region. Many low-caste villagers are extremely poor and have little or no opportunity for advancement. Villages remain in a cycle of poverty. We help church leaders reach out with care and the compassion of Christ to meet practical needs: clean water wells, nutritious food, literacy and skills trainings, and so much more.

Empowering pastors creates ministry that spans far beyond a temporary list out of difficulty. IGL pastors are equipped, trained, and resourced to meet needs with accountability and a person-to-person approach.

Each pillar serves and is supported by Indian believers, who by the world's standards are considered poor. Yet true to the mechanism of God's economy, they find themselves overflowing with joy in the midst of suffering, strengthened by gratitude, and privileged to be significant in the real and eternal Kingdom. The first pillar, of course, is church planting and evangelism. As villages are reached with the gospel, we come alongside them with the blessings of medical assistance, aid to children, and economic development resources.

Kavita
MEDICAL OUTREACH

First, I'd like to introduce you to Kavita. I've known this young woman for many years. As a young girl, she came to live on the Sharon Campus where my wife, Prati, and I have our home. Kavita's mother passed away when she was five, and her dad found himself unable to care for his three daughters. He brought them to our children's home and asked if we would raise the girls. Of course, Kavita missed her mother very much. Over time, though, she came to feel that her home at the Sharon Campus was a true home for her. She felt known, and seen, and cared for.

Just recently, she told me that now as a college graduate, she is looking back at her time at Sharon with fresh eyes. "It was only in this home that I had an opportunity for an education, and, as a young woman, I had the safety and security I needed to grow." She reflected, "The greatest treasure, though, that I received in this home is that

I got to know Jesus as my personal savior. When I came here as a child, I had no idea at all about God. But here, I learned about Jesus. He is my treasure." Today, Kavita has graduated from college and is back at Sharon Gardens where she is putting her education to use as a nurse at Sharon Hospital. We are so blessed that she decided to come "home" and share her own abundance with those in need.

Kavita now works as a nurse at the Sharon Hospital.

Chitra
ECONOMIC DEVELOPMENT

My daughter, Becky, oversees an initiative we call Women's Transformation Groups (WTG). The goal of these groups, which focus on the same rural areas that our church-planting efforts do, is to give women a solid financial and economic education. After participants complete a six-month program, then they are encouraged to start their own business and are eligible to receive a loan to that end.

Women gather to learn about banking, entrepreneurship, accounting, and auditing at a WTG.

Becky met Chitra at a WTG micro-credit loan class not long ago. Chitra had not completed schooling because her high school was a great distance away from home, and Chitra's parents didn't feel that it was worth risking her safety to walk to school. So she stayed home. She was married relatively young, at eighteen, which is not uncommon in rural India. What is uncommon is that she was not able to have children. Chitra shared that as a woman in poverty, with no education, no skills, and without children to care for, she felt insignificant and trapped. All the while, she very much wanted to be a contributor, to be "a somebody," to be significant.

The day that Becky met her, Chitra was stopping by a WTG to receive a micro-credit loan. It was her third! With her first, she'd purchased a sewing machine. After building a tailoring business in her village and paying back the initial loan, she was awarded a second loan so that she could expand her business. She purchased a second sewing machine. Now, she had paid back the second loan and was receiving a third with the two goals of taking her business to the production level and opening a training center for other women. She now trains and employs women in her village.

In the middle of all this industry and energy, Chitra was able to become a mother! Ten years into her marriage, she had a daughter, and, a while later, a second little girl. Chitra has big dreams for her beautiful girls and for the women in her village. She confided to Becky that her hope is that the other women in her village, and especially the younger women, would have the freedom to make choices and could make positive impacts on the people around them.

Chitra felt trapped and alone, but with what she was given, she's now giving to others.

Jabez
CARING FOR THE SICK

On May 1, 2016, the world lost a young evangelist and prayer warrior named Jabez. Many visitors to Sharon Gardens campus, which is my home and home to Sharon Hospital, remember the young boy, who could always be spotted cheerfully greeting patients and visitors alike.

Jabez's life was difficult from the start. As a baby, his parents abandoned him at Sharon Gardens. While this seems cruel, they were most likely hoping to connect him with care that they would never be able to offer. He was diagnosed with cerebral palsy and spina bifida. Jabez underwent several corrective surgeries but was confined to a wheelchair for the remainder of his life. Despite this, his physical limitations never stifled his joy and capacity to impact others for the Kingdom of God.

There wasn't a single person who came to the hospital who wasn't touched by the words, prayer, and witness of this young life. His exuberant joy was both contagious and unforgettable. In the brief fourteen years of his life, God used Jabez to leave a lasting impression on hundreds of lives.

Jabez has been a great blessing to me and my family—far more than we could have been to him. Jabez taught all of us at Sharon one simple yet profound lesson: God has placed a divine seed in every human heart that, when exercised well, always produces the capacity and space to love others.

If Jabez had lived longer, we would have only loved him more. Yet, God loves him far more than we ever could, and we know beyond a shadow of a doubt that Jabez is now walking, jumping, dancing, and rejoicing in God's presence!

In rural India, a child born with any kind of disability is destined for a life of dependency. Disabled children are often considered social and financial liabilities. For the extremely poor families who live in these areas, the financial strain associated with any kind of care is an insurmountable reality. In addition, rural families have a very limited understanding of children with special needs. These children do not go to school and hardly leave their homes. Most of them are also severely malnourished, for families often favor a healthy child over a disabled child and dole out food and attention accordingly.

Families lack access to standardized screening and diagnosis, let alone any kind of intervention or support. Without awareness, access, and resources to care for children with special needs, these children are left in the direst of circumstances.

The Children's Wellness Center

Largely inspired by our years with Jabez, in 2016 we opened the Children's Wellness Center at Sharon Gardens. Today, we are caring for thirty children with various special needs and offering them therapy, rehabilitation, and counseling. It is the first of its kind in Salem, which is a city of almost 1 million. We hope that our Children's Wellness Center can be a model for the care and well-being of special needs children. Our vision is that these children would have hope for the future—not just for survival, but for abundant living.

Called to Be a Witness

Andie, Erin, Neil, Kavita, Pastor Benjamin, Chitra, Jabez, and many more—these brothers and sisters are beautiful witnesses of God's power in weakness! Because they have been faithful with a little, the Lord has entrusted a great work to them. I see their examples as both corrective and encouraging. Corrective, because the handcuffs of materialism have captured the Western church almost to the same extent as they have the culture. Encouraging, because these humble brothers and sisters are living generously despite youth, weakness, poverty, and limitations. They are experiencing joy, peace, and power. And I know you can too. Growth comes from giving.

But as we'll see in the next chapter, joy, peace, and power will not be ours if our goal is to stay safe or to remain "intact." Growth happens in movement.

REFLECT

1. When it comes to your finances, time, gifting, education, career, home, and other resources, do you tend to have an "owner" or a "steward" perspective?

   On a scale of 1–10, 1 being "My stuff is mine, and I decide how it is used" and 10 being "Everything I have is God's, and I look to him for how he wants me to use it," how would you rate yourself?

   1   2   3   4   5   6   7   8   9   10

2. Sometimes we need a "reality check framework" with which to evaluate our hearts. Respond to these questions and consider what the answers reveal.

   a. In this past year, would you say you have grown in love for and generosity toward God's Kingdom, or are you growing more focused on loving and spending on your own Kingdom?

   b. Where is your time invested? After making a chart of how it is used, evaluate its effectiveness as a commodity that you can give to others.

   c. Describe a time when you received and, out of joy and gratitude, gave back.

3. Ann Voskamp summed up the message of the feeding of the 5,000 by saying, "The bread that we give to feed another's soul is what miraculously feeds ours." How is God nudging you to serve and give sacrificially? Maybe even foolishly?

   a. Share this vision with other believers in your fellowship and take steps toward giving to build his Kingdom.

   b. Do you trust that he will take care of you as you undertake these endeavors? (See Matthew 6:31–33 for additional encouragement.)

CHALLENGE

But even if I am being poured out like a drink offering on the sacrifice and service coming from your faith, I am glad and rejoice with all of you. So you too should be glad and rejoice with me. (Philippians 2:17–18 NIV)

1) Do you understand the kind of joy that comes from sacrificing for a worthwhile cause? Ask the Lord to show you what sacrifice could look like in your own life and share his answer with a friend.

2) What differences between the temporary and eternal perspectives do you see at work in your life? Where is God trying to shift your priorities from temporary, earthly comfort to eternal, lasting glory? What uncomfortable steps is he encouraging you to take?

KINGDOM VOICES

Rev. Vasantharaj Albert
Vice-President of the Non-Denominational Association of
Interdependent Churches (NAIC)

We want to encourage churches to look outside the church rather than looking inside the church in order to become unleashed agents for community transformation. The church needs to address some of the issues such as poverty, disease, and illiteracy.

Today I was talking with a medical doctor who is an expert in community development, and he told me that the World Health Organization says that one of the important reasons for poverty is the medical expenses that people incur. So once people are in the loan trap, the cycle continues, not only to that generation, but to the next two or three generations.

India is a place where God has given such a lot of natural resources. There is no reason for people to live in poverty. They've been exploited and don't have the skills to use the natural resources that God has given. But once the church is involved in the community, the discipleship process really accelerates development because believers get involved in the problems of the people who are not inside the church. So people in ministry here are trying to think of how the church can best do that. That's a huge challenge before us—to be a kind of value addition to the people who live in the community.

chapter 8

GROWTH HAPPENS IN MOVEMENT

Chapter 8
Growth Happens in Movement

My church describes itself as a movement. It doesn't like to think of itself as a denomination. But it is a denomination. Once, though, it was a movement, back in the 1880s, when it began. This church originated as a reaction against the institutional church, in fact. The people wanted to be disentangled. They were creative, innovative, didn't carry any baggage, were not protecting any traditions, and were not protecting any history. They had no stories that began, "My grandmother taught me this in Sunday School." They were people who were completely unhinged from what had happened before, save their commitment to what they understood to be a biblical experience of Jesus.

The lead guy at that time was creative and willing to take a risk. He started an evangelistic newspaper; he used a riverboat to travel from town to town on the Ohio River, preaching to people along the way. He died in 1895, prematurely—he was only in his fifties. Within two generations of his passing, people were trying to preserve—to codify—what he did. He had a newspaper? We've got to have a newspaper. He traveled on a riverboat? We've got to travel on a riverboat. These methods were in play until at least the 1950s. I think he would spin in his grave if he knew what had happened to his "movement."

This story, which my dear friend Jim Lyon shared with me, is an insightful—and unique—example of how movements become institutions. There is a certain trajectory to human endeavors: infancy, activity, exploration, growth, maturity, building, accumulating, slowing, and finally death. By the end of this journey, we are often so weighted down that movement is impossible. The gravity and pull of the world lead to heavy stagnation.

Keeping a Movement as Movement

So how do we keep a movement *as movement*? Is it possible? Selvasingh Watson, another good friend of mine, is involved in indigenous church planting among oral tradition people groups in India. He says that the question for this movement is whether their children and their children's children will be able to push against the gravity of a heavy, self-focused institution. Candidly, he suggests that the Western church may serve as a cautionary tale, a lesson for the infant Indian church—a case study of which we may ask, "What happened in the West, and how can we avoid it?"

Of course, this is not a recent or modern problem. The history of the church at Ephesus tells us this. In Paul's letter to them, it's clear that while they faced typical human problems and struggles, they were a vibrant church. Paul says, ". . . ever since I heard about your faith in the Lord Jesus and your love for all God's people, I have not stopped giving thanks for you, remembering you in my prayers" (Ephesians 1:15–16 NIV). Yet later in the book of Revelation, we read that the same church, the church in Ephesus, had lost its "first love." It had already become an institution.

> I know your deeds, your hard work and your perseverance. I know that you cannot tolerate wicked people, that you have tested those who claim to be apostles but are not, and have found them false. You have persevered and have endured hardships for my name, and have not grown weary.
>
> Yet I hold this against you: You have forsaken the love you had at first. Consider how far you have fallen! Repent and do the things you did at first. If you do not repent, I will come to you and remove your lampstand from its place. (Revelation 2:2–5 NIV)

The people of this church were doing a good job of defending the faith; they had little tolerance for bad theology; and yet their fervor—the soul of the work—was lost. At the same time, they were losing their first love. They were building hierarchy, structures, and developing a clergy/laity distinction; and that institution squeezed out life.

I talk to my leaders and my people often about this. We are twenty-five years into this movement—close to one generation, with the second generation now beginning to rise up. The question of "how do we keep a movement as movement?" is a real one with real consequences for us.

Focus on the First Line

When I was a child, we had to learn to write in cursive. Good handwriting was very important. My teacher taught me something that has stayed with me all these years. She would write one sentence in flawless cursive at the top of each page. We were to copy that line ten or twenty times. At no point in the exercise were we to refer to the previous line that we'd written. We were only to look at the first line, the original. Over and over and over, our reference point was the first line, the forerunner, the standard.

It is so, so important that we keep going back to the New Testament for our references and models. It is here that we see Jesus, our forerunner and standard. It is in the scripture that we watch the growth of the church unfold, study Christ's character and choices, understand his Great Commission, and are challenged to obey the greatest commandment. Our team intentionally talks about this all the time. It is a paradigm that must be instructed.

My friend Jim (of the riverboat church movement) says this, "Jesus is the subject. We have to constantly strive to make *Jesus* the central idea, not the church. When the church becomes the central idea, we begin to conflate the way of Jesus with the way of a church." We need to teach Jesus as the first line of reference. We want our people looking back at him, not at what we "wrote" in the last generation. Everything should be based on that first line, and each believer should be unleashed to see what their particular "handwriting" looks like as they endeavor to follow Jesus.

If the human trajectory moves from growth to gravity, then the spiritual trajectory is almost its opposite. In the spiritual realm, growth starts when we die. How's that for an upside-down principle? Death is the way to life—active, vibrant, directional life—and this growing, in-motion life always produces a great harvest.

Discipleship Is the Pathway to Spiritual Life in Motion

So what does life in motion look like? Is there really a pathway away from stagnation, heaviness, and institutionalism? I'd like to suggest that the scripture provides us with a powerful picture of the way to keep movements moving, and that is discipleship.

"Discipleship" has come to mean many things. Some churches organize large "discipleship" classes in which hundreds of people are walked through a curriculum, and at the end of eight weeks they are considered discipled! Perhaps they even receive a certificate to indicate that they have "completed" discipleship training. I am not taking issue with developing a knowledge foundation. Knowledge acquisition, however, is not the same thing as discipleship, and it is to our detriment if we think it is.

In the rest of this chapter, I want to first show you how discipleship is integral to keeping movements in motion. Second, I want to paint a robust, scriptural, doable picture of what discipleship looks like in the unleashed church.

Discipleship Is Always Relational

Discipleship isn't a word or a concept that originated with Jesus or in the New Testament. Jesus' audience and the early church audience would have understood discipleship from a broader cultural construct. They would have known that discipleship is always relational. Both first-century Jewish rabbis and Greek philosophers had disciples, and everything that they taught or passed on happened while the disciple, or learner, was following them around. Literally. Both the teacher and his disciple went to work, ate meals, and walked the public square together. They celebrated as families together. I believe the modern phrase is, "they did life together."

We have an intimate view of what discipleship looked like with Jesus and his friends. Or shall I say, Jesus and his disciples? (Either works because his disciples *were* his friends!) They slept around campfires together, went fishing together, got chased out of wheat fields together, fed crowds together, went to synagogue together, and prayed together. And yes, we know that Jesus' disciples even had a tendency to fall asleep while Jesus or a fellow disciple prayed, which demonstrates another aspect of discipleship—they were close enough to hurt each other. This kind of real-life proximity meant that Jesus risked disappointment and pain by investing so deeply and personally. Pain, disappointment, great joy, significance, and love— these are always part of "real" relationships. These are always part of "real" discipleship.

Relationship conveys so much more than curriculum ever could. Relationship communicates ethos. (*Ethos* means "character," and it is used to describe the disposition and core values of a specific person or community or movement.) There's a popular English phrase that describes how ethos is transferred: "caught, not taught." I think we instinctively know that there can be a significant gap between what a person says and how they live their lives. Discipleship infiltrates that gap. Rather than simple knowledge acquisition, discipleship allows learners to "catch," or take in, the whole of a person's life lived with Jesus. It's a worldview transference. It's a life transference.

In 1 Corinthians 11:1, Paul says to the believers, "Follow my example, as I follow the example of Christ" (NIV). Ultimately, all believers are to get their life, purpose, beliefs, challenges, comforts, significance, direction, and love from Christ. As we are animated, or made alive, in relationship with Jesus, we pass life along, living out what it looks like to be conformed to his image.

Discipleship Is Always Purposeful

We humans seem to love swinging from one extreme to another, don't we? I understand that there is a segment of Western Christianity that has understood and embraced discipleship as relationship. And this is good. This is very good. It seems, though, that discipleship as relationship can sometimes swing too far, becoming instead "discipleship as hanging out"—or as we say in Tamil, "*chumma*." Jesus loved time with his disciples. They were, as we said earlier, his friends. But Jesus and the New Testament authors saw discipleship as purposeful and always working toward a goal. This was an "understood" in the first century. As a matter of fact, to some extent, discipleship and apprenticeship were the same thing. The teacher, or rabbi, would teach, train, and do. The learner, or disciple, would learn through instruction, observation, imitation, and application.

Proclamation and teaching can be done in a crowd. "Admonishing and teaching with wisdom" require the kind of closeness that comes with biblical discipleship. The goal of it all—the instruction and the personal application—is that disciples become "mature in Christ."

Scripture describes two primary purposes, or outcomes, of discipleship. I would argue that they are so closely linked that they are actually one. They are maturity and love.

> He is the one we proclaim, admonishing and teaching everyone with all wisdom, so that we may present everyone fully mature in Christ. To this end I strenuously contend with all the energy Christ so powerfully works in me. (Colossians 1:28–29 NIV)

Like discipleship, the concept of maturity in Christ is probably lost in translation. What does maturity mean in this context? Does it mean old rather than young? Does it mean serious rather than silly? Paul extends our understanding of "mature" in 1 Timothy 1:5 when he writes, "But the goal of our instruction is love from a pure heart and a good conscience and a sincere faith" (NASB). Maturity is the goal = Love is the goal.

Just before Jesus was arrested, and right after he'd washed his disciples' feet, he gave them this instruction: "A new command I give you: Love one another. As I have loved you, so you must love one another. By this everyone will know that you are my disciples, if you love one another" (John 13:34, 35 NIV). How will people recognize

Jesus' disciples? By the size of their Bibles? By the fact that they go to church? By bumper stickers they sport on their cars? Read those words again: "By this everyone will know that you are my disciples, if you love one another." Love and maturity. Love = maturity. This is the purpose — the ultimate goal — of discipleship.

Discipleship Teaches Us to Trust and Obey Jesus

Jesus described the mechanism that moves us toward love and maturity when he famously authorized his followers to "Go . . . and make disciples of all nations, baptizing them in the name of the Father and of the Son and of the Holy Spirit, teaching them to observe all that I have commanded you" (Matthew 28:19–20a ESV). So we are to teach disciples to obey Jesus—to follow close behind him, to do what he does, to go where he goes.

Jesus says that love and obedience go hand in hand: "If you love me, you will keep my commandments" (John 14:15 ESV). Why is this? I believe we've often misconstrued Jesus' words to mean that we must somehow "prove" our love for him by being as obedient as we can be, by toeing the line, by following the rules. This, however, leads to an inordinate focus on our behavior and a diminished focus on the person of Jesus.

To throw another wrench into the whole thing, scripture clearly teaches from front to back that the *only* thing that pleases God is faith—trusting him. So we're to teach people to obey Jesus, but the only thing that pleases God is faith?

If we step back for a moment and work to connect the dots, I think we'll see what's happening between obedience and love and maturity and faith. A call to follow Jesus means, quite literally, to go where he goes. Obedience is responsiveness to Jesus. It means saying yes when we might be afraid, or tired, or ill-equipped; it means saying no to our own inclinations when Jesus tells us he has something better in store. It means following along on the walk to Calvary. It means loving God with all our heart, soul, and strength and loving our neighbor as ourselves.

There is no true obedience, there is no walk toward Calvary, without faith. When we trust that Jesus is good, even with just a mustard seed of confidence, then we find our hearts more inclined to obey and follow, more inclined to love. As we increasingly count on his sovereignty, his victory, his wisdom, and his intimate love for us, we will obey more quickly and more readily. Our obedience looks like love: we will love more quickly and more readily.

Discipleship teaches us to obey all the things that Jesus taught us. As we do this, we are transformed—we mature—into people who love God and love our neighbors as ourselves.

Good Discipleship Is High Investment/Low Control

A church on the move—the unleashed church—succeeds because it is formed in relationship rather than founded on rules, rituals, or religion. Relationship is dynamic. A church that grows out of relationship will be dynamic as well. The basis of this kind of dynamic relationship is a vital relationship with our life source, Jesus Christ. Healthy, "alive" churches grow as the life of Christ is poured out in love, through good discipleship.

And what are the distinctives of good discipleship? High investment and low control. Let's talk about what these distinctives mean. First, what do I mean by high investment? In Philippians 2:17, Paul says he is being poured out like a drink offering. Paul says he is running, laboring, mothering, fathering—being poured out for his people. That's his role as a discipler. It requires a high investment in others and death to self. It means valuing others above yourself. It's not looking to your own interests but, instead, to the interests of others. It's having the same mindset as Jesus, who "made himself nothing by taking the very nature of a servant" (Philippians 2:7 NIV).

Next, what do I mean by low control? In the same passage, Paul describes what the disciple is responsible for, and then how God is involved. To the disciple, he says, "Work out your own salvation with fear and trembling . . ." (Philippians 2:12 ESV). The disciple is responsible before God to walk in awe, faith, and dependent obedience. Undergirding that faith-walk is God's work. He is working in the disciple. He is shaping the disciple's desires and empowering him or her to do what pleases the Father. This is what I mean by low control: a discipler is not responsible to shape anyone's desires nor to "make" him do things that please the Father, and a discipler does not "figure out" how their disciple should work out his salvation. Good discipleship looks like a Jesus follower pouring out his or her life for another Jesus follower, trusting God to shape that person's heart and to empower him as he works out his own salvation before God.

I see four aspects of high investment/low control discipleship relationships, and because I'd like this material to be practical rather than theoretical, I'm going to take the time to dig into them a little. I hope you find this useful.

1) Principles > Practices

Principles are deep, wide, and flexible, while practices are narrow and specific. A discipler who teaches Biblical principles will pass on love and godliness rather than methodology.

Let me tell you about my friend Janelle. Janelle lives in Seattle and is discipling a woman who has moved to the States from Thailand. Janelle is American and is from a Christian background. Her disciple is Thai and is from a Buddhist background. They couldn't be more different in terms of religion, culture, and language. So how much control should Janelle exert to shape what her disciple's faith looks like? How many strategies, curriculums, and evangelism methods should she teach her disciple?

Janelle's work is to lay out Biblical principles and to teach her disciple how to interpret those principles in light of her own historical, cultural, and social background.

Why don't we take a moment to explore how we might disciple around principles rather than methods? In 2 Peter chapter 1, Peter describes the character of a person who is able to love effectively, the character of a person who knows Jesus in such a way that their life has become effective and productive because of it.

> For this very reason, make every effort to add to your faith goodness; and to goodness, knowledge; and to knowledge,

self-control; and to self-control, perseverance; and to perseverance, godliness; and to godliness, mutual affection; and to mutual affection, love. For if you possess these qualities in increasing measure, they will keep you from being ineffective and unproductive in your knowledge of our Lord Jesus Christ. But whoever does not have them is nearsighted and blind, forgetting that they have been cleansed from their past sins. (2 Peter 1:5–9 NIV)

Peter exhorts us toward character without delineating a three-step plan to get us there. He doesn't say, "Here is what goodness should look like for you. This is what kind of knowledge you should obtain and what curriculum you should use to get it. You need to be more self-controlled in these areas, and I suggest you approach it in this way." Instead, he lays out a foundational principle: that if a believer is struggling to grow in these areas (faith, goodness, self-control, love, etc.), it is most certainly because he is "forgetting" what Christ did on the cross. There is power in remembering. There is power in meditating on the gospel, in preaching it to ourselves every day, in remembering our "before" story, and rejoicing in our new story. There is power for character change and power to love effectively.

Digging into potent foundational principles such as the one in 2 Peter 1 is at the core of good discipleship. The principle of "remembering the cross" is taught and caught, and it can be teased out in all kinds of life circumstances, in every culture, from spiritual infancy until "that day" when we are presented mature in Christ. A person who has been trained in godly principles, and trains others to that end, will introduce generational longevity to their work. Godly principles are at the core of flexible, Spirit-following people and of responsive, Jesus-centered, "moving" churches.

2) God's Word Is Not Chained

Some time ago, I was reading through second Timothy, and the beginning of that chapter seemed to jump off the page. What I saw there revolutionized my thinking about how I approach God's truth.

It says, "Remember Jesus Christ, raised from the dead, descended from David. This is my gospel, for which I am suffering even to the point of being chained like a criminal. But God's word is not chained" (2 Timothy 2:8,9 NIV). Read that last sentence again: "But God's word is not chained."

Paul recognized that he was limited, restrained, and finite—"even to the point of being chained like a criminal." But he wasn't without hope. Why? Because he understood that the word of God is in no way weak, in no way bound, but is, in fact, free to act with power upon the hearts of those who have ears to hear. Just a few sentences earlier in his letter, Paul says to Timothy, "Reflect on what I am saying, for the Lord will give you insight into all this" (2 Timothy 2:7 NIV). Isn't that interesting? Paul's job was to speak. Timothy's job was to reflect. God's job was—and is—to give insight.

Remember, powerful discipleship is high investment and low control. When we approach discipleship in this way, we have a high investment in reading, studying, talking about, and sharing the word of God. We have low control over how, after a person has studied and reflected, they gain insight into the scripture. We can count on God for that.

So why are we afraid to allow people to read the scripture and hear from God themselves? Paul wanted Timothy to have the liberty to reflect and the liberty to apply the scripture as the Lord gave insight. Could we relinquish control in the same way? Why do we feel we need to do the work of the Holy Spirit? Why don't we believe that God still speaks through his word today? The only clear reason is that we must think that the gospel is chained.

Some of you may not like what I'm about to say, but do you know how I see the gospel and the word of God chained today? I see that it is chained in the frameworks and by-laws of denominations and restrained inside institutional models and by rules, accreditations, and certifications. It is chained by the clergy/laity divide—structures that prevent eager believers from taking their places in the body of Christ. Please know that I do not disparage or have a problem with theological training or seminaries. We need those, just as we need standards of education.

Ask yourself, though, how the institutional model applies to a church like the indigenous church in India, which is growing exponentially. If every church planter had to go to seminary before he or she could preach the gospel, the bottleneck would soon choke out organic growth. You know, this problem is exactly what the letters to the seven churches in Revelation address. In the letter to the church at Sardis, Jesus said, I see you doing all these things "right." You have the reputation of being alive. You have all the degrees and certifications. You are doing "the things." But you are dead.

God's word, however, is living and active. It remains *unchained.*

3) Prayer Is Ground Zero

In many ways, the heart posture of prayer is a picture of what it means to be high investment and low control. Paul talks about "devoting" ourselves to prayer, "laboring earnestly" in prayer, praying with a sense of alertness. You can't get much more high investment than devotion, earnest labor, and a fully engaged mind. Jesus snuck off to pray as often as he could, praying through the night sometimes, and sweating blood at the end. As disciplers, our prayer time is ground zero. Spiritual battles are fought here. Our anxieties and fears are submitted and replaced with gratitude and confidence. The will of God is discovered. Doors are opened for the gospel.

The truth is, the more we invest in prayer, the less likely we will be to try to control any outcomes or to control our disciples. Prayer frees us to watch and wait for the Spirit to act and gives us confidence to jump in when we see him move. (If you tend to have controlling, anxious behavior, ask yourself if it is because you are not resting in God's love and power through prayer.) Good discipleship is grounded in prayer.

Good discipleship apprentices prayer. Our disciples want to copy us, want to be like us, and therefore it is oh-so tempting to present ourselves as the person with all the answers. Apprenticing in prayer—praying for our disciples, praying with our disciples, allowing them to see into our personal prayer life as well—equips them with something much more substantial and powerful than any of our wisdom or answers. By praying with our disciples, we teach them the foundational truth that we are weak and he is strong, that we come with empty hands and he supplies all, and that our job is to ask, watch, and wait. When we pray with our disciples, we teach them Jesus is a person, not a concept; that his mercies are new every morning; and that gratitude builds a life of contentment.

It's impossible to outline all the treasures that you'll pass on to those you disciple as you apprentice in prayer. It's impossible because what you're actually doing is teaching them to draw near to Jesus, the author and perfecter of our faith. He is the immeasurable, only wise God, full of love and compassion, the source of resurrection power. There is nothing stagnant about a connected relationship with Jesus and nothing institutional about discipleship that is rooted in prayer. Surely this is one of the ways that movements keep moving.

4) Disciples Are Doers

The final aspect of high investment/low control discipleship is that disciples are doers. Since we've already discussed this in terms of apprenticeship in this chapter and under "Leaders, Stop Doing Everything" in chapter 5, we'll just touch on it briefly here. I'd say that a clear litmus test for whether you are practicing low-control discipleship is whether or not your disciples are beginning to do the things that typically you have been responsible for doing.

Recently I heard about a small group in the States that had been meeting together for years. At a certain point in time, the leadership in the small community shifted, and this change revealed some troubling dynamics. While high-investment discipleship had been happening—in some cases, for half a decade—the younger believers had not been released to "do" anything. The leader did all the teaching rather than training and equipping others to teach. The leader did all the planning rather than tapping into the abilities and aspirations God had entrusted to the body. The leader did all the "understanding" rather than encouraging individuals to seek God and to grapple with him in the word and prayer.

Teaching and training that never results in doing is a fast track to stagnation in the body of Christ. They must increase, and you must decrease. This is hard. But the joy of seeing younger believers exercising their gifts and taking their place in the body of Christ is well worth it.

Can Movements Keep Moving?

There has been much discussion and scholarly research regarding the stages of movements. The general consensus is that human movements cycle through predictable stages, and that they will always wax and wane. I am not suggesting that our indigenous church movement in India will be the first to break this mold. Why pose this question, then, about whether movements can keep moving? Why write this chapter?

I'm asking these questions and writing this chapter because there is something incredibly hopeful and absolutely real moving through history, weaving its way through time, never flagging, never aging, only growing and increasing, sowing life and harvesting even more. This is the movement of the Kingdom of God. I suppose we could say that the movement of the Kingdom of God has "predictable stages of growth" too. It is predictable that the Kingdom has come and will come, bringing with it life and flourishing.

Let me be clear. Our hope is not that any particular movement will "crack the code" and last forever. (And that's probably a good thing, because knowing us humans, we'd want to take credit for it.) Our hope is in the work of the Holy Spirit, who "blows wherever he pleases." He is like the wind. John tells us, "You hear its sound, but you cannot tell where it comes from or where it is going" (John 3:8b NIV). God—immortal, invisible, wise—is dynamic, always moving, and building his living Kingdom, bringing life to all who enter into it.

At the beginning of chapter two, I told you about the Chicago church that closed its doors after sixty-four years. I'd like to share the rest of the story with you. My friend Dave Ferguson is the pastor of Community Christian Church, a planting church with ten locations in Chicago. One of them is right around the corner from the closed church. Recently, he and I were talking about this idea of movement in the church, and Dave described it in terms of the life cycle of a living organism. He suggested that just like all living organisms have a life cycle, so do individual churches and movements. They are born, develop, mature, reproduce, and die.

"[None] of the churches that Paul wrote to in the New Testament are still around," Dave noted. "You know," he continued, "I'm leading a church in Chicago. We have ten locations and thousands of people, and that's awesome. The grim reality though is that the same thing that is true about me—that someday I'm going to cease to exist and I'll die—is true about this church. Having that understanding is a bit of a paradigm shift. We have to think in terms of legacy, not of longevity."

This idea of legacy versus longevity has been forming in Dave's mind for a while, but it was that closed corner church in Chicago that cemented it for him. You see, before they closed the doors for good, the board of elders asked Dave if he would meet with them. He told me he was a little reluctant to go in the midst of his dense schedule, but because he knew they were good people who really wanted to help the community and proclaim Jesus, he headed over one morning. He says:

> So I go in and sit in this room, and it's seven or eight old, I mean really old, white guys. You can imagine the scene. All of a sudden, the meeting shifts from what I expected. The guy who's the chairman of the elders says, "You know, we've been going through the book of Acts, and we really feel that the vision of church is multiplication and planting churches, and we're not doing it. And we don't have a younger generation.
>
> "We could keep doing what we're doing right now for another ten years, since we have a little bit of money in the bank, and we're still beating our budget." [But] then, one at a time, they went around the room, and they said, "You know, we decided that we want to close the church and we want to sell the property, which will net about $2 million. And we want to give it to two different church planting organizations, because we feel like what's best for the Kingdom is for us to actually go and sell our property. [We want the proceeds] to be used to plant other churches."

And I mean, I had to repent. This was ridiculously bold faith to say, "Okay, we've had a good run, we've been around since the '50s." They had 120–150 people, so they were actually larger than a typical church. They had money in the bank. And they weren't going to shut the doors tomorrow. But they could see the future, and what was the best use of their resources. So they sold the building. They gave to two church planting organizations, and that money has helped to plant churches all over the place. I want to tell their story, because I thought it was such a bold move to understand that it's about legacy and not longevity.

Just like the wise leaders at the corner church, you, too, can tap into the movement of God's Kingdom. You can go along for the ride. You can watch for Kingdom activity, work where God is working, teach your disciples that your trust is in him and not in what you build, hold lightly to walls and structures, and hold tightly to Jesus himself.

Moving Christward

People have always been drawn to Jesus—or they've tried to crucify him. Either way, he has always been someone to be reckoned with. Today, just as in New Testament times, we are seeing people drawn to the person of Jesus Christ and to the power of the Holy Spirit. In India, we are simply saying, "Here is Jesus. See him in action, hear him in his word, experience him in your personal lives, find salvation, be redeemed. And here, too, is the Holy Spirit. He is sent to guide you, to comfort you, to teach you, to guide you into all truth." We point people to Jesus and release them to follow him in the power of the Holy Spirit. Our job is to provide the peripheral support that they need to move and multiply. Christ himself is making all things new. Our hope is in him, and in following him. Jesus is on the move–let's keep close behind.

Right now, IGL is pouring everything we've got into what God is doing in the villages of India. He is working there; his Kingdom is being established; the harvest is plentiful. As you will see in the next chapter, we are witnessing the Kingdom expand village by village as agile, responsive, discipling, reproducing churches grow and flourish. The Kingdom is on the move, and it cannot be stopped. Let's take a look and see what God is doing.

REFLECT

1. Everything we do should be based on the "first line" with Jesus as our central reference point. What do you think that first line principle looks like in your life? How might your "lines" reflect traditional church culture instead?

2. A disciple is responsible before God to walk in awe, faith, and dependent obedience. How do you see God growing you in each of these areas?

3. Reflect on the believers with whom you meet regularly (at least once a week). Would you consider any of those relationships discipleship relationships as described in this chapter?

4. I have talked in this chapter about "low control/high investment" discipleship. In which of these areas would you like to ask God to help you make some shifts? (Circle any that apply.)
   a. from high control toward low control
   b. from low investment toward high investment

5. Take a moment to describe what you think this shift might look like.

6. As disciplers, our prayer time is ground zero; it's how we fight spiritual battles. How much of your time is spent in prayer *for* your disciples? If you struggle in this area, consider keeping an active prayer journal or prayer cards for each of your disciples. Jot down one idea of how your prayer for your disciples could improve, and ask God to help you toward that end.

7. How often do you pray *with* your disciples? When you pray with them, do you reflect all aspects of your own faith walk, characterized by humility, repentance, faith, dependence, and thanksgiving? Are you vulnerable about your fears, weaknesses, and struggles? If not, why do you think that is?

CHALLENGE

For those not currently in a discipling relationship (being discipled or discipling another), consider the following questions:

> And Jesus came up and spoke to them, saying, "All authority has been given to Me in heaven and on earth. Go therefore and make disciples of all the nations, baptizing them in the name of the Father and the Son and the Holy Spirit, teaching them to observe all that I commanded you; and lo, I am with you always, even to the end of the age" (Matthew 28:18–20 NASB).

1. We often read the above passage as a call to share the gospel of Jesus Christ. Sometimes, however, we miss the command to disciple new believers, teaching them to observe (and live out!) Christ's words. Based upon this chapter's definition of discipleship, what is the biggest challenge for you in making this change? What hindrance is in the way of starting a discipleship relationship with a fellow believer?

2. In your walk with Jesus, do you have a desire to be discipled? If you desire to grow and be challenged in this way, ask the Lord to bring an older believer in your life who would be willing to "do life together" with the goal being Christ-centered maturity and love.

For those who are currently discipling, consider the following questions:

"You therefore, my son, be strong in the grace that is in Christ Jesus. The things which you have heard from me in the presence of many witnesses, entrust these to faithful men who will be able to teach others also" (2 Timothy 2:1–2).

1. Write down a list of the kinds of things you hope to entrust to your disciple. In addition to teaching your disciple, what do you think it looks like for you to model what an animated, vibrant, Christ-centered life looks like? How, specifically, would you like to see your disciple, in turn, reflect those things to others in their life?

2. As this chapter pointed out, discipleship is relational and purposeful. In what ways are the people you work with moving toward and building purposeful discipleship relationships of their own?

KINGDOM VOICES

Dave Ferguson
Bestselling Author and Founding and Lead Pastor of Chicago's Community Christian Church

Jesus didn't say, "Go and plant churches." He said, "Go and make disciples" (Matthew 28:19). At the same time, he said to go to "Jerusalem, Judea, Samaria, and the ends of the earth" (Acts 1:8). So how do they go from where they are to making disciples to Jerusalem, Judea, Samaria, and the ends of the earth? I think his vision gets some legs and strategy when Paul, who was a church planter, comes along and gives his instructions to Timothy in 2 Timothy 2:2. He says, "Hey, this is going to start with you, Timothy. But then it's going to go on to others; we're going to teach others." So, in some ways, I think we have this vision that Jesus gives us of disciple making and also the multiplication in Acts 1:8, but then we get the strategy from Paul in 2 Timothy 2:2. So church planting and discipleship are completely integral to one another.

I think movement is important because movement is how you accomplish the mission. And the only way you get to movement is multiplication. And you don't get to multiplication unless it happens at the discipleship level. So, you have to be constantly making disciples. And then some of those disciples are going to have leadership gifts. And so, what they do with those leadership gifts is they begin to start different forms of *ecclesia*, different forms and expressions of the church. And as they start different forms and expressions of the church, those churches do what churches do when they're working well—they form other disciples. And so, the only way you ever get to movement and multiplication is by starting with discipleship.

Steve Moore
Former Executive Director of Missio Nexus, Executive Director of nexleader

We have a significant misunderstanding, or flaw, in our understanding of discipleship in the West. My experience is that we've thought about discipleship from a very linear, and at sometimes incomplete, perspective. So commonly, in North American Christianity, when you talk about discipleship, the first thing that comes to mind is the idea of spiritual formation and the things that need to happen in the life of a Jesus follower for them to develop godly character and pursue a sense of intimacy with Jesus, which is very important, of course.

The problem is, we tend to view that personal spiritual formation in isolation, separated from what I would describe as ministry formation. And because we think of spiritual formation in isolation, we have wrongly developed a "knowing based" understanding or definition of spiritual maturity. So your spiritual maturity is defined by how much you know—about the Bible and even about what you're supposed to do to fit into the framework of how we do church. That's a really incomplete and incorrect understanding of spiritual maturity.

I think biblical spiritual maturity, the kind that Jesus talked about, is not based on how much you know but, rather, on how big the gap is between what you know and what you do. And so, the smaller the gap between knowledge and obedience, the more mature the person is. That weirds out North American Christians, because when you think of spiritual maturity in that context, a person can be mature for their age in Christ, knowing very little about the Bible, as long as they're actually doing almost everything that they know.

In a global context, where the church is growing most rapidly, spiritual maturity is often through discovery Bible studies, where the focus is on Dallas Willard's two important questions of discipleship: What is God saying to you? And what are you going to do about it? So it's linking knowledge with obedience. And my premise is that when the gap between knowledge and obedience is small, spiritual power tends to be high. When the gap between knowledge and obedience is large, spiritual power tends to be low.

I believe that one of the things that mystifies Western believers about the Majority World church is how people who don't even know the four Gospels can go pray for someone and see them healed, or can cast a demon out of someone in their village, or whatever it might be. But, again, this goes back to my premise: where the gap between knowledge and obedience is small, that's where true, spiritual power tends to be high.

chapter 9

GOD IS AT WORK:
STATS AND STORIES

Chapter 9
God Is at Work: Stats and Stories

The Kingdom of heaven is disrupting Satan's tightly held infrastructure. In India, those of us on the ground see freedom and unprecedented flourishing erupting all around. The Holy Spirit's movement to unleash the indigenous church has changed the very way that we "do" the Great Commission—and to miraculous ends. I want to invite you into that. I thought I'd share a snapshot of what we're seeing by way of some stats and stories. Be encouraged! Though our task may seem overwhelming, God is at work, and he is winning.

THE WORK AHEAD OF US

If we were to take a flyover view of India, one of the first things we might note is the sheer number of people living here. Were we to move in a bit closer, we'd see scores of religions, hundreds of people groups, and hundreds of thousands of villages. All of this makes introducing Jesus to millions who have never heard his name seem a daunting task, indeed! For perspective, consider India's population and land mass compared to that of the United States. This juxtaposition alone is jaw-dropping. Take a look at the numbers in the graphic on the following page.

Today India's population is over 1.3 billion people. *Billion!* Compare that to the population in the United States, which is just over three *million* people. It can be difficult to even conceive of the magnitude of difference between millions and billions. If you have trouble wrapping your head around it, the formula above of seconds versus days versus years may help. But let's not stop there. Let's compare the size of both countries by placing India on top of the US. Again, mind-boggling. Now imagine if four times the number of people living in the United States were suddenly transported to a country half its size. And you thought US cities were congested!

India THE WORK AHEAD

Understanding Millions & Billions

1 Million Seconds
12 DAYS

1 Billion Seconds
32 YEARS

United States Population
329,201,263

India Population
1,369,862,502

1,000,000,000+ People in India belong
to an **UNREACHED** people group

That's **1 out of every 7** people on earth

Now let's look at how many *unreached* people there are in India: over one billion. That number doesn't mean the other 370 million are Christians. No. It just means that 370 million people have *heard* the gospel message at some point. One billion people in India are still totally unreached. That's one out of every seven people on earth. One out of seven! On the entire earth. When you look at it through the lens of the Great Commission, India suddenly becomes far more important, doesn't it?

Take a look at the graphic that follows, representing people groups, villages, and religions.

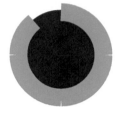

People Groups
2,585

UNREACHED
People Groups
2,311

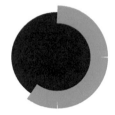

Total Villages
600,000

UNREACHED
Villages
360,000

80% Hindu

11% Muslim

7% Other

2% Christian

2/3 of India's Population Lives in Rural Villages

780
Languages

10/50
EXTREME

Ranking in countries where Christians face the most **persecution**

Notice, first, that nearly all of the people groups in India are unreached. Well over half of the villages are unreached. And, as of today, Christians make up only 2 percent of religious people in India and are highly persecuted. Clearly, this illustration paints a picture of the mountain of work we have ahead of us. But God. He is working. He is moving mountains to establish his Kingdom in a predominantly Hindu country that seems to want no part of him. Other religions can't hold him back. Language barriers can't hold him back. Persecution can't hold him back. He won't stop until every single person has been reached. Until every single person has the opportunity to know him.

Why? Because God loves India. As difficult and heartbreaking as the realities are in India, God will never stop pursuing his people. Let's take a look at some of those realities:

POVERTY	EDUCATION	HEALTH	SAFETY

270,000,000 Indians are poor (living on $4.30 per day)

45% of poor are illiterate

21% of poor have access to latrines

63,400,000 rural poor lack access to clean water

100%
of India Gospel League's
work is in rural areas

80%
of India's poor live
in rural areas

27%
of the population lives
in urban areas

Crime against
women went up

↑**200%**
between 1995
and 2017

75%
of healthcare
infrastructure is in
urban areas

Heartbreaking and difficult indeed, isn't it? When we see numbers like this, we aren't even sure how to crack the surface of a problem this big. But we can't lose heart. After all, it's God who is in charge here. He is at work, and we must trust that he is in control.

He wants to see India's people come to know him in a real and transforming way. He wants the poor to come to him. He wants the sick to come to him. He wants the uneducated to come to him. He wants the abused to come to him. And he has called us to help with this great task. He has called us to serve. To give people access to clean water. To give them access to jobs so they can provide for their families. To give them access to healthcare. But most of all, to share the Good News of Christ so that people have access to the comforter of all comforters.

God has already done so much in India, and he will continue to. Let's take a look at how he is moving mountains. (This graphic is based on our data up to the end of 2019.)

GOD
IS WORKING

100,000

Churches planted

1,850,546

People baptized

100,000

Villages reached

7,398

Pastors trained

2,213

Women leaders
trained this year

3,748

Youth leaders
trained this year

Churches are being planted, people are being baptized, rural villages are being reached, and leaders are being trained! And these numbers only represent the work of India Gospel League! There are many other organizations sharing the gospel and winning souls for Christ.

While winning souls is our top priority, IGL doesn't stop there. We also want to raise people up and enrich their lives. Take a look at the graphic below based on our data for 2019.

GOD
IS WORKING

14,200
Bibles distributed
this year

1,558
Women who
received a
micro-loan this year

108
Water wells built this
year (total built as
of 2019: 400)

3,657
Children cared for
by IGL this year

1 million
Children attending
CGCs this year

13,279
People cared for by
IGL medical programs

What does raising people up and enriching their lives look like? For us, it looks like giving people clean water to drink, giving them access to healthcare, providing a way for women to contribute to their families, and serving children in our communities. Because when people are cared for, when they are healthy and flourishing, they can then give to the flourishing of others.

This is God's Kingdom at work. This is God's church disrupting Satan's tightly held infrastructure. This is God on the move in the hearts and lives of his people.

STORIES OF GOD'S GRACE AND REDEMPTION

We've just dug into numbers, stats, charts, and graphs. Sometimes a robust understanding of what is happening in our world can only be delivered through that kind of mile-high, big-picture view. And it is exciting, isn't it? As Christians, though, we know most profoundly that every single human "data point" is, in fact, a precious, loved, created person born with a capacity to know the eternal God. Our hearts are so much more than switches that toggle to "Jesus-follower" from "not Jesus-follower." We toggle, if you will, from "dead" to "alive," and it's this life—organic, changing, moving, growing, blossoming—that can never be fully described by data.

Some of the best hours of my day are when I walk Sharon Campus in the evening. It's a beautiful place. I wish you could see it. Cool plaster buildings in pink, peach, and white offer wide, shady porches and patios. Fragrant gardens overflow the worn paths. Macaques, a genus of Old World monkeys, argue in the trees.

Solitary walks in this lovely space are a treat for me and many others, but it is not the solitude that draws me. In the cool of the evening, when school has ended for the day and work is winding down, I can walk outside and be with people. I stop along the way and talk with children, teenagers, nurses, teachers, entrepreneurs, Bible teachers, staff, neighbors, brothers and sisters, seekers, and students.

Days when I'm not at Sharon Gardens, I sit down with village people, grassroots pastors, women who are kicking off new business ventures, men who have come to know Christ and are being restored to dignity and purpose. This is my joy. I love this life God has entrusted to me. The great treasures of my life are people, rich with the capacity to know and be known. I imagine that many of you feel the same way that I do.

As long as the government allows it—and my guess is it will be no more than a year longer—I extend an invitation for you to come to Sharon to meet my family and friends. You'd love it. You really would. God is doing amazing things here. (The food is delicious too.) In the meantime, I'd like to introduce you to some of the precious people with whom I get to walk, talk, and fellowship with every day. Jesus has changed their lives, and He is overflowing in their lives to bring life and flourishing to others. Let me tell you their stories.

Stephen's Story

Candlelight flickered, illuminating heavy, acrid smoke as incense wound its way around a table covered with idols and icons. Stephen sat in front of them, crouched and fearful. He did this every day. As much as a teenage boy could be, Stephen was committed to doing *poojas*— the daily rituals of Hinduism. He lit candles, broke coconuts, and offered flowers, water, and food to pictures of goddess Mahakali, hoping to stave off the feelings of guilt and fear that weighed him down at night. His family believed that they could see the divine in those photos, and that through the images, the goddess might be watching them.

Stephen's parents weren't particularly devout. Even so, several times a year during celebration times, they took a goat to a temple near their home and offered it to the priest for forgiveness of their sins. Would that be enough to ease the anxiety and dread? It didn't seem like it. Most nights, Stephen went to bed afraid of the punishment that the gods might have in store for him.

In the daytime, it was a smell that made him feel afraid. His dad would stumble into the small house, slurring, tripping, and muttering until he collapsed on a chair. Alcohol and sweat swirled in the air, announcing the chaos and despair that followed Stephen's dad everywhere he went.

That day, as Stephen knelt in the flickering light, he wondered, "Will this ever change? Can my life ever be different?"

If Stephen were a statistic, we'd see that the likelihood of his growing up to repeat this cycle of defeat and destruction was high. In a nation of 1.3 billion people, who would care about this frightened, ill-fated boy?

The small cement house in Chandrapur was already hot with sun; sounds of traffic, animals, and chatter wafted through the window. Stephen's mom was at his side, shaking him out of his last minutes of Sunday sleep. "Get up," she ordered. "We're going to church." Stephen's face registered with sleepy confusion. He would not have been more surprised if his mother had announced that they were getting up to go to the circus. Dressing quickly, a million questions swirled in his mind. Not last on the list was, "What do people wear to church?" Stephen stepped out of the doorway and was surprised— no, shocked—to see that his father was also up, dressed, and apparently headed to church too.

They left the house and wove their way through a press of people, *tuktuks*, and motorcycles on the dusty streets until they turned onto a familiar street and stopped at a familiar house. "Namaste!" called Sharad, Stephen's father's good friend, who had invited the three of them to accompany them to church. Sharad and his family stepped out onto the street, and together the group proceeded to twist and turn through the crowds until they finally arrived at a plain white block building. It was indiscriminate except for an emerald green door and a talkative throng of brightly dressed, smiling people outside.

Encountering Jesus is life changing. And that day, in that little church, three of the 1.3 billion people in India encountered Jesus— and for them, nothing was ever the same again.

Stephen's dad was the first to trust Jesus. His addiction had wreaked havoc in his life, and he desperately wanted to be free. Jesus set him free and gave him new life. Gentle, friendly, fearful Stephen watched with amazement. He was hearing about Jesus for the first time ever. He was watching his dad's life be restored, transformed, and redirected. But mostly, Stephen told me, "I was amazed by Jesus' love and his sacrifice. Who is like Jesus? Who would die for human sins?" This Jesus was nothing like the scrutinizing, punishing, and distant gods and goddesses who seemed to want so much and to give so little.

Stephen's mother put her trust in Jesus next, and after watching the transformation in his father's life, Stephen did too. "I never thought I would be a Christian or a servant of God, but the Lord made me his child. I encountered God when he delivered my father."

Today, Stephen lives with his wife and three kids in Ghugus, about twenty-five kilometers away from his childhood home. They are busy! Together, they run a children's home and help to manage a nearby Bible college. Stephen teaches at the college, equipping young believers to plant and lead churches. Stephen, who once dreamed of being a movie star or an army general, now dreams of building a home for elderly widows and other aging people without family.

As he reflected on the past nineteen years of knowing and serving the Lord, Stephen told me, "I have felt called to serve needy people and love them the way the Lord loved me. It's my pleasure to share God's love with other people. I thank God for using me in his vineyard and making me a blessing to others—my passion is for Christ and his work."

Yes, this is Jesus' way: rescuing, restoring, and releasing people so that they, too, can be part of God's great rescue mission. I'm so grateful for my brother Stephen and his family. He is gentle, friendly, and now, instead of being fearful, he is a significant worker in the Kingdom.

When we last spoke, Stephen asked me to pass something along to you. "I'm thankful that you got to hear about me." Just so you know, this isn't a statement made of out self-focus or aggrandizement. It's the humble thrill of a person who once was lost and now is found, basking in the knowledge that he is loved and known by God the

Father and now by many brothers and sisters across the sea. He also asked that we pray for his family, his Bible school students, and the children who live in the home on campus. "Please pray that the Lord will grant us his wisdom and knowledge so that we can do his mighty work effectively." Yes, indeed. Let us pray that for Stephen.

R. Shanthi's Story

The granddaughter of a Hindu high priest and the daughter of a priest, R. Shanthi spent days, weeks, and months bowing to idols in her home, fasting regularly, and trekking to the local temple with her family to worship their gods. Both of the temples in her small village of Mettupatti were unique and revered. They were three hundred years old and built in the shapes of pyramids. These temples were the center of village life and even drew adherents from miles around for bi-monthly *poojas*. Her devout family hosted many rituals and festivals in their own home as well so that her grandfather could preside over them.

Although it seemed that Shanthi was completely surrounded by and steeped in Hinduism—something she now describes as darkness and blindness—the Good News of Jesus was breaking in.

Many of Shanthi's childhood days were spent indoors in bed. She was sick all the time. Of course, her parents worried for her and prayed regularly to their idols for healing. When she was about nine years old and in the fourth grade, she was sicker than usual. Nothing was helping, and her condition worsened with each passing day. Her parents were doing everything that they could to appease the gods, but it seemed they were not listening, didn't care, or weren't able to help. They began to lose hope in these gods.

At the same time, a relative of Shanthi's came to visit. He prayed to the Lord Jesus to heal Shanthi and suggested that Shanthi and her parents also pray to him. He said that they should "trust Jesus." Shanthi's parents hung on his words and onto the hope that perhaps this Jesus would do something for their dear child. They prayed to Jesus. Miraculously, Shanthi was healed. The family immediately left their old customs and turned toward Jesus. Looking back on this time, Shanthi said, "We acknowledged that he is the true, living God who listens to what we ask. This miracle drew us to Christ and helped us start to trust him."

Around the same time, the *Jesus* film was screened in Mettupatti. Shanti learned that Jesus was crucified and hung on the cross to pay for her sins. She started thinking about Jesus every time she had a quiet moment. Inside her heart, she acknowledged again that he is the only true and living God. At just nine years old, she decided that she would follow this living Jesus and would live her life for him as well.

A church had been planted in her village, and Shanthi and her family joined the community there. Even at such a young age, she was deeply impressed by the stories she heard of how Jesus was changing lives. When Shanthi told me her story, she recalled how hearing those stories specifically overwhelmed her with Jesus' unconditional love and his faithfulness to answer prayers. "I was reaching for Christ, and I fell in love with him."

The same relative who had originally visited during her sickness visited her family with Bibles, Bible stories, and songs. He gave her family a Bible as a gift. Shanthi's family devoured it. They began to read, starting with the birth of Jesus and continuing all the way through to his death and resurrection. This was a turning point for the whole family. Together, everyone claimed Jesus Christ as their personal savior and trusted him for their salvation.

Some relatives turned against them, saying that they were abandoning tradition and trading it for a foreign god. Shanthi's father stood in calm strength against them, determined never to go back to the empty, dark, fear-infused religion of his ancestors. Shanthi was glad to stand behind her father's strength and determination; she and her sisters began to gather regularly to pray for all of their relatives and to ask Jesus to save them too.

Now, as an adult with a family of her own, Shanthi says that the biggest miracle she has witnessed is the transformation of her family. God was faithful to answer the prayers of that little girl, and, now, many of her family members have turned to Christ and trusted him.

"I feel called to serve, love, and give," Shanthi said. "I feel very satisfied to share about Jesus' love with other people. It is good for me to share God's love." Shanthi feels that God has fulfilled so many of her dreams. She'd always wanted to be a teacher, and she was able to work in a daycare for ten years. She loves to help people and wants to see the community change, and the Lord has positioned her in a micro-credit community organization. She hopes for a great revival in India, and she is now working for IGL as a grassroots Adopt a Village Coordinator, building relationships and connecting new villages with the life transformation of the gospel. She requested that I ask you to pray with her for several potential church plants in other villages.

Shanthi gave her life to the Lord and entrusted him to guide and use her as he saw fit. And what an adventure she's been on ever since! I want to close Shanthi's story with a quieter adventure, but a beautiful one nonetheless. When we last spoke, Shanthi wanted to tell me about her dearest friend, a woman whose name is also Shanthi.

> I have a close friend named J. Shanthi. When we met, I was so surprised that she had the same name as mine! She and her husband are involved in ministry just like my husband and I are. Whenever we talk, we find that our thoughts and words are similar. She shares things with me that are much the same as what I think—our thoughts are aligned. We are true friends in Christ, since we love each other, share each other's burdens, and pray for each other too. She tells me that I am the person whom she can trust for anything and everything in her life. I thank God for her.

Praise the Lord who reaches into the darkness to seek and save a little girl. Praise the Lord who sets us free to be significant. Praise the Lord for tender love and friendship. What a beautiful thing he has done for and through our sister Shanthi.

Dayal's Story

"The Lord saved my life from the pleasures of this world and made my life meaningful to others." Isn't it an amazing salvation that frees us from slavery to trinkets and recreates us as people of eternal significance? This is Dayal's story.

If we were to talk with Dayal's friends, they would describe him as a joker, a food lover, and a flexible guy. He is fun-loving and easygoing. They would also tell us that he is a person who has learned to love people with Christ's love, patiently and deliberately walking alongside them as they learn to know Jesus.

As a child, Dayal was awakened by his grandfather every morning for a ritual bath in the river, which was followed by a visit to a nearby temple to bow before statues and icons of their gods and goddesses. His grandfather was a Hindu priest, and the entire family took great pride in their religious status and dedication to the temple. All the while, though, Dayal lived in fear of not measuring up. Punishment and even death awaited those who didn't worship often enough or well enough. The gods and goddesses demanded his best, and Dayal wasn't sure he could offer it.

A family of Christians lived in his neighborhood in Ranchi, a city of over one million in the state of Jharkhand. Dayal noticed that their lives and lifestyle seemed different from his and his family's. Dayal began to spend more and more time at his friend's house, and the family shared the gospel with him. He heard about Jesus for the first time.

All of it was interesting and intriguing, but Dayal's initial conclusion was that Jesus was a foreign god and wasn't right for him. As a kid trying to be a good Hindu, he couldn't ever imagine himself as a Christian.

Several years went by, and at the end of high school, his Christ-following friend gave him a Bible. Dayal started reading and was struck by Jesus' power to mend, set free, and give peace. Satanic bondage, illness, and alienation were broken and healed at Jesus' hand. He said, "I started reading and found the truth." He was drawn near. Through reading the word of God, Dayal said, he personally experienced Jesus' love and divine peace. He confessed his sin and worshipped Jesus as the one true God, his personal savior.

Since then, of course, he's been on an adventure with Jesus. His family members strongly disapproved of his decision to follow Jesus and demanded that he drop it. He began to pray that one day they too would come to the Lord.

A godly man named Ruael began to disciple him, walking him through the early days of his faith. Initially Dayal said he found it hard to love people with the boldness and patience of Christ. Sharing the gospel was nerve-racking, and the disappointment Dayal felt when people rejected the gospel was severe. But the Lord molded him. Recently he told me, "As a child of God, I am very happy to share God's love and to love people." What a beautiful thing!

Dayal is still fun-loving and still likes to eat, especially his wife's mouth-watering mutton biryani. And today, God is using this friendly, even-tempered man in significant ways. His entire family has come to Christ, and they too consider themselves witnesses and ambassadors for Jesus. Dayal is discipling another man, Sunil, and loves getting together with him to talk about Jesus, purpose, and eternal life. He prays that Sunil will also be light in the darkness and will teach other men to be disciples of Jesus.

Dayal asked that you pray for him—that he would do the Lord's work faithfully and play his part in building the Kingdom of God. Dayal is eager to be part of church planting in the unreached villages in his state. He says, "Thank you for hearing about me."

God Is Working and Winning

I imagine that *we* are the ones who are thankful to have heard about Stephen, Shanthi, and Dayal. Yes, the spiritual movement in India right now is wild, miraculous, and unprecedented, but it is all happening one person at a time, through precious souls like these. It is clear that

Jesus loves them so much. He is breaking chains, setting the captives free, bringing them into his fold, and then spilling out his love and grace through them to other people. May our hearts never grow cold to stories like this—stories of radical heart change, stories of hope, stories of eternal significance. This *is* the way of Jesus.

Jesus' way is not different for you than it is for these men and women living in Indian villages on the other side of the planet. He wants to capture and radically transform your heart. He wants to be your hope. He offers you significance. God is working, and he is winning—here and there. How are you responding to his disruption in your heart? In your church? May he disrupt our "stuck" places and lead us on that wild ride of following Jesus.

You can be a part of God's victorious work in India, you know. I want to tell you how in the next chapter.

REFLECT

1. In this chapter, we read three stories that demonstrate God's relentlessness in setting captives free. How was your view of God challenged?

    a. How did you react to these stories? (Were you amazed, doubtful, bored, etc.?)

    b. Why?

2. When challenged to evangelize, we can feel paralyzed by the great task before us! When you think about reaching out to others with the gospel, does your reaction tend to be one of hopelessness or one full of hope?

    a. How does God fit into your reaction?

    b. In all three stories, how did God work creatively and sovereignly to save each person?

    c. We learned how God saved an alcoholic, the grandson of a Hindu priest, and a sick little girl—all in middle-of-nowhere villages.

    d. What specific things can you learn about God's character and his approach to people from these stories?

3. Is God pushing you to share his love with a person or a community you may have written off as too far gone or too difficult? How might what you learned about God's character and his approach to people in India inform how you interact with that person or community group in your country?

4. In the West, you may get discouraged about slow growth, as more people are turning away from God than turning toward him. Take a minute to reflect on these stories. What are some stories, big or small, in which you've seen God working miraculously to change lives and bring people to himself?

CHALLENGE

> *For he has rescued us from the Kingdom of darkness and transferred us into the Kingdom of his dear Son, who purchased our freedom and forgave our sins. (Colossians 1:13–14 NLT)*

1. What is the Kingdom of darkness? Think about people you know: how are they trapped in this dark Kingdom? How do you see God's light shining in their lives? How do you see God's rescue mission at work?

> *No human wisdom or understanding or plan can stand against the Lord. The horse is prepared for the day of battle, but the victory belongs to the Lord. (Proverbs 21:30–31 NLT)*

> *Yours, O Lord, is the greatness, the power, the glory, the*

victory, and the majesty. Everything in the heavens and on earth is yours, O Lord, and this is your Kingdom. We adore you as the one who is over all things. (1 Chronicles 29:11 NLT)

2. No doubt, you trust that God is the victorious king, leading the charge to set captives free. Where is the evidence of this happening in your life, family, friends, community?

KINGDOM VOICES

Becky Stanley
Director of Children's Ministries, India Gospel League

I've always been intrigued by the passage in the Gospel of John where Jesus calls the first disciples. John the Baptist is standing with his disciples when Jesus passes by. John tells them, "Here's the Lamb of God," and the two disciples hear him and immediately follow Jesus (1:35–40). I think a good disciple maker is one who points his disciples to Jesus to make disciples for Jesus.

So how do we do it? We do it not just by education. We are working in a very illiterate or semi-literate context in the rural villages of India where people are just coming to Christ. One way is, of course, teaching, training, and educating them—helping them understand what Jesus' teachings are and how to live like Jesus. We don't want to just talk about these principles. We want to answer the question: How do you actually live like Jesus?

These churches are planted in rural communities where there's abject poverty, there's physical suffering, there's all kinds of injustice, there is oppression, there is darkness, there is pain—all just right there in front of your eyes. So how can this person who is now a follower of Jesus Christ actually *be* a disciple in this context? We teach them what it means to love, what it means to express Christ's love, what it means to express his mercy. So the story of the Samaritan, for example, is not just broken down as a theological study, as a curriculum. It's actually taught to be lived out. And this is what Jesus would do.

chapter 10

WHAT IS GOD DOING NEXT?
ACHIEVE 2040

Chapter 10
What Is God Doing Next? Achieve 2040

In my country, there are over 600,000 villages in India, and somewhere between 1,600 and 1,800 unreached people groups live in those villages. To date, we estimate that indigenous churches have already been planted in 200,000 of those villages. But we believe there can be a church in every single village in the next twenty years. Is this an outlandish goal? An unreasonable vision? Maybe. But we serve a BIG God who is uniquely igniting India for himself right now. We want to be part of that movement. We want to see the church unleashed to work where God is working.

A Wild Ride

Since 1992, we have been on what can only be described as a wild ride. Back then, we felt that God was leading us to do something different than we had done in the past—something big. After much prayer and discussion, we set a goal of unleashing two hundred church planters who would commit to planting 1,000 churches by the millennium. It felt like a huge stretch. An impossible dream. But it was a goal made in faith, and we entrusted that big dream to an even bigger God.

Over the next eight years, more and more indigenous believers were raised up, eager to join in wherever they could—serving the least of these, making disciples, and planting churches. Back in 1992, if we would have received a word from the Lord saying, "Buckle up. We're about to take off!" I'm not sure I could have imagined what would happen next. But in those eight years, the Lord used ordinary men and women to plant not 1,000 but 20,000 village churches! We were stunned.

Our plans needed an update. (God obviously had more in mind!) In the next ten years (by 2010) 40,000 more churches were established in previously unreached villages, which amounted to 100,000 village churches planted since this movement of God began in 1992. Praise the Lord. Other Christian ministries are excited about this work too. As a result, our latest estimate is that between 200,000 and 250,000 village churches have been planted in India.

Some twenty-five years later, in the latest "update" of God's call, he's given us another bold goal: to work toward having a church in *every village in India* in the next twenty years! I like acronyms, so we're calling this ACHIEVE 2040: **A Ch**urch **I**n **E**very **V**illag**E**.

I actually believe that this goal is perfectly reasonable, given the pace, scope, and nature of what God has been doing in my country. IGL envisions planting 200,000 additional churches (double the number planted in the last twenty-five years); and we believe other ministries will plant churches in the remaining 200,000 villages. It is a real possibility that we could reach all of India with the gospel in the next twenty years! Buckle up, indeed.

Our God is an awesome God, and in the past twenty-five years, his Spirit has moved over India in ways we could never have imagined, eternally changing the hearts of millions. He has also used his Spirit to shape my heart and the ministry of IGL. He has been growing us not only in size and scope, but in depth of understanding. We are twenty-five years better equipped to disciple, to multiply, and to saturate India with the Good News. He's used the past twenty-five years to get us ready for the next twenty. We are excited and ready for this leg of the adventure, whatever it may hold.

Listen to this story of how the principle of multiplication works.

Pastor Rao left his village on foot and headed into the mountains of tribal Andhra Pradesh. Although he had only to walk two kilometers, he would soon enter a cluster of villages so remote that they didn't know that they shouldn't drink the same water in which they bathed and washed. The people foraged rather than farmed, and they barely wore any clothing. They certainly had never heard of Jesus Christ and his love for all people. Pastor Rao had been praying for these villages and praying for this trip long before he set out. That day, full of faith and Good News, he walked briskly despite the hot sun and difficult road.

He entered the village area and began to explain his presence there to the curious people who met him on the streets. He explained that he was there to tell them about a God they didn't know—the one true God who had come to bring peace. As news spread, a crowd gathered, and in the crowd were a group of young men. These men were wielding thick sticks. In a flurry of visceral anger, the men converged on Pastor Rao, beating him and chasing him out of the village. They warned him that if he returned, they would not beat him—they would kill him. The young men believed that if Pastor Rao were permitted to speak about his God, their gods and goddesses would leave their village. Their anger was really rooted in a deep and ever-present fear of punitive spiritual forces.

Injured and beat up as he was, Pastor Rao developed an even deeper burden for the lost tribal people in those mountains of Andhra Pradesh. Back at home, he prayed earnestly for them every day.

Eventually, one of those frightened, angry young men came down the mountain in search of Pastor Rao. He entered Rao's village and asked where to find him. A villager brought the young man to Pastor Rao, and they sat down to talk. The young man told Pastor Rao that ever since he'd been chased out of the village, a mysterious sickness had fallen over the tribe. The people began to think that they had been cursed. Desperate to appease their gods and goddesses, they'd offered sacrifices and pleaded with them to lift the curse. It made no difference. Eventually some of the people began to wonder if perhaps they were getting sick because they had rejected Pastor Rao's message.

"Please forgive me for beating you!" begged the young man. "Please forgive all of us!" Of course, Pastor Rao was glad to forgive this enemy for whom he labored in prayer each day. He was also overjoyed to say yes when the young man asked if he would return for a "do-over" and another try at telling them about his God.

The two of them left immediately for the mountain villages. When Pastor Rao and his new friend arrived, a crowd gathered, and the pastor announced the Good News of Jesus Christ. Thirty-five of the forty families in the village accepted Jesus as their personal savior that very day.

The new believers began to gather as a church, and over the next year, the village experienced an astounding transformation. Before, the people were oppressed, blinded to their own potential and the opportunities around them. They lived in poverty. They did not cultivate the land. Disease ran rampant and unchecked. Women were regarded as sub-human. Many villagers were lost in addiction to alcohol. Their lives were without hope.

The church—the body of Christ—has been a life force and a beam of light in the darkness. The vibrant village church has made it possible for the village to be part of IGL's "Adopt a Village" program. Development initiatives such as healthcare, education, skills training, and agriculture training are in place. These transformative initiatives all point to self-sustaining practices within five years. God's Kingdom is come in this village, where hope, love, and justice are now a way of life.

A Church in Every Village—It is Possible

Over half of all Indians live in villages. Some are very small, with fewer than five hundred residents. Others are sizable, with populations up to 10,000. No matter the size, each village typically centers around a temple, and the people there worship a local deity. Villages may or may not have electricity, even though every Indian village technically has access to a power grid. Many villages do not have easy access to clean water. There are usually government school buildings in every village, but the presence of a school building is not a guarantee that there will be a teacher. Villages are most often Hindu, but some are Muslim, and others are tribal. In fact, some of the villages we serve are so remote that they are yet unreached by Hinduism!

I believe that every village, no matter how small or diverse, can be reached with the gospel by 2040. I offer four strategies and explain how each one is working for us in India: through the village church, through discipleship and equipping, through saturating, and through networks. This is exciting stuff. And while there are some ways in which their use is particular to India, I believe that it would be wise and interesting for my Western friends to consider how these principles might work in their context. Jesus is relational, and his church is primarily a relational organism. Relationally based, saturating church growth should be something we can see anywhere, even if not in the exact same way. As you read these principles, consider how they might be adapted for use in your own church.

I can't really say this is a "typical" village,
since India is so vast and so diverse,
but it is an example of a remote village.

Through the Village Church

If you've been involved with Christian missions at all in the last couple decades, you've heard lots about unreached people and unreached people groups. Unreached people groups are distinct cultures (differentiated by language, religion, music, clothing, etc.) in which fewer than 2 percent are Christians and have heard the gospel. A specific way to describe and define these people groups has been evolving ever since Donald McGavran and Ralph Winter, missiologists and church growth pioneers, started talking about *ta ethne* in the mid-20th century. *Ta ethne* simply means "people groups," and we hear the words in this familiar call, "Go into all the world and preach the gospel, making disciples of all nations," or making disciples of *ta ethne*—all the people groups.

Once Winter and McGavran began to talk and write about *ta ethne*, the idea caught on in the West, and soon mission agencies were identifying and describing people groups, eager to make progress on the Great Commission by focusing on reaching them with the Good News of Jesus. And this was good. But the whole thing was and still is complex and nuanced. Missiology groups identify people groups in various ways, resulting in diverse numbers and descriptions. Of particular challenge are people groups that have scattered for one reason or another. They are identified as one people group, yet in each of their specific "new" locations, they are shaped by distinct cultural climates and circumstances, and so their receptivity to the gospel is not standard.

The reason I'm saying this is that the strategy of reaching people according to their groups has not really been effective, except in specific cases. In India, the village is a powerful entryway to the lives of *all* the people. The unreached peoples are living within these individual, often very rural villages. And while a people group may have migrated across a wide area, each of the villages have a distinct cultural footprint. Each village creates its own unique culture and its own network of relationships. Bringing the gospel through the gates of individual villages allows indigenous church planters and pastors to circumvent some of the cultural difficulties.

When IGL sends church planters and pastors into the villages, we do not send "missionaries," per se. Rather, we identify people whom God has raised from that particular culture or from a culture group with a close affinity to it. Those indigenous believers, through organic connections in the village, introduce the gospel to the people there. If even a small handful of people are receptive to the message of Jesus—if even two or three are gathered—then they begin to meet as a church.

The church in every village effort is not about "addition based" church planting. We aren't rallying 1,000 church planters to head out to 1,000 villages and plant 1,000 churches. Rather, the idea is that every church reproduces itself. We're talking about multiplication, something exponential. This is where things really begin to get exciting! See the comparison in the graphic that follows.

Addition-Based Church Growth

Addition-based church growth is focused on adding people to one particular church body. Usually, this "accumulation" strategy relies on a few charismatic leaders, is focused on programs and events, and values pouring resources into growing the church hub. Members are

typically not mobilized, gifts are under-utilized, and much of the growth is "transfer" growth rather than new believer growth.

Multiplication-Based Church Growth

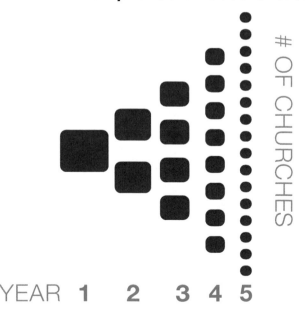

Multiplication church movements happen when churches plant churches. These communities are invested in raising up leaders and workers who are ready to deploy and plant new groups. "Ordinary" believers are considered workers, and there is an ethos of high engagement.

Through discipleship and equipping, IGL pastors raise up leaders who can either replace them as they go out to start a new church or who can go out themselves.

Through Discipleship and Equipping

Healthy multiplication happens in one way—through robust discipleship. I've seen this played out in the relationship my wife Prati and I have with Prem and Lillian, a couple we've known for over twenty years. When we met Prem and Lillian, they were newlyweds living in a tiny hut in an undeveloped, remote village. A distant relative of mine told me about this couple—Prem, a mechanical engineer, and Lillian, with a master's degree in nutrition—who had resigned from their jobs and headed out into the villages of the Dharmapuri district to share the gospel.

Prem and Lillian had a burden to share the gospel and were acting on it. In terms of spiritual growth, they were established believers and highly educated people. They could grow spiritually. We didn't have to sit with them and go over a Basic Christianity curriculum as we do with many of the other people with whom we work. These two were zealous, but they were young, new to ministry, and new to family life. What they needed was support, encouragement, and a model of what it looks like to live out a diligent, long-suffering life of sacrificial service. Prati and I related to them as a family. We built a relationship. We prayed for them.

Just a few weeks ago, Prem and I were reminiscing about those early days, and he told me, "When you met us all those years ago, we were not known beyond the tiny village where we lived. And we did not know how to make ourselves known." Discipling Prem and Lillian meant helping them look beyond just the two people that they were. It meant giving them a vision to raise up not mere converts, but disciples who "owned" the vision and were just as zealous, sacrificial, and eager to reach the lost as Prem and Lillian were. It meant modeling what that looks like. In order to unleash the indigenous church there in Dharmapuri, Prem and Lillian needed to raise up disciples who could raise up disciples.

Prati and I cast a vision, but as Prem noted in our recent conversation, we also trusted this young couple with real responsibility. "You didn't wait to entrust us with significant responsibility until we were 100 percent able, had 100 percent of the skills, and were completely mature," he recounted. That's right. We didn't hold out for that. Why? Because more than we trust the competence of any man, we trust the power of God to work through those who are willing.

Eventually, India Gospel League was able to support Prem and Lillian's work by providing a Life Center in their village. Our discipleship relationship was woven through with prayer, modeling, teaching, encouragement, friendship, and practical support.

All these years later, Prem oversees not only an entire region of churches that are part of the India Gospel League network, mentoring dozens of pastors, but he also mentors the regional coordinators for four other regions! Lillian helps to lead our Women with a Mission team, which unleashes thousands of women every year to take the gospel message out to their own villages. What the Lord has done with two people who once could not imagine a reach beyond one tiny village!

To plant churches with multiplication DNA, we must multiply at the individual level, which happens through discipleship. IGL wants to see the gospel spread organically from person to person, village to village, not in big rallies, nor by sending cross-cultural missionaries. That's why equipping the local church is of such high value. An incredible amount of our energy goes into equipping the church to witness to its own community, impact it, and then to reproduce itself.

Through Saturating

Life-giving, other-centered, equipping discipleship leads to healthy, flourishing, growing churches. Once even a small church is bubbling with this kind of vitality, then it is primed to send off workers to a neighboring village. Again, we're not sending cross-cultural missionaries. We're not sending people to an entirely different culture with which they're not familiar. That's the old missionary model. Instead, we're following natural relational and cultural connections: we're sending folks to the village over the mountain where their second cousins live. They can enter, they can communicate, and they can carry the gospel over existing bridges.

As relational discipleship and church planting moves out incrementally from village to village, following natural pathways, we begin to see entire regions become saturated with the gospel. Our goal is to focus on equipping and strengthening these local churches so that they are able to spill out spiritual life all around them. If we had a map of India and placed a pin in every village where a church was planted, I'd expect to see gospel saturation around each pin. Slowly but surely, the gospel would spread out geographically. Again, this is not an addition model of "sending." Instead, we are strengthening local churches so that they become life-giving and reproducing.

The goal of saturation informs IGL's regional approach to reaching the unreached villages. A region is comprised of a limited number of people groups, ethnic groups, and languages. Sometimes only one language is spoken in a region; sometimes a couple of languages may be spoken if there are two or three tribal or ethnic groups in the area. Regional efforts keep our work from becoming overly complex. We're not learning new languages, eating new foods, or trying to understand a new culture. Believers are working among their own people. Even when they saturate out from their own villages, they are more culturally, socially, and economically similar, and hence, they are more likely to be accepted.

To speak specifically, let's say we were to make a goal of planting one hundred churches in a region. We'd identify strategic villages—villages where people are responding to the gospel—and equip them to gradually grow, multiply, and enlarge that geographic area with more churches who have multiplication in their DNA, until a church is planted in every village.

Through Networks

It was 1989, and I was sitting in the JFK Airport in New York waiting for a flight. Something new was happening in the airline industry, and the buzz was everywhere. The very first airline alliance was unfolding about that time. At a very basic level, two airlines were sharing information, collaborating, and while remaining discreet, were joining forces to provide better service to their passengers. They were building a network that would allow the airlines to offer *together* what they would never be able to offer alone. I sat in that airport restaurant and thought, *It's an amazing idea that these airlines are getting together to form this group. They'll be able to maximize their investments, skills, and abilities. Imagine the potential!*

At this point in time, the concept of networking was not common currency. Of course, today we unconsciously think in terms of networks because of the ubiquity of computer networks and the world wide web. Back in 1989, though, the idea of these airlines networking together to leverage what they each offered represented a radical change in how they had been operating. It kept running around in my mind. As I waited for my flight, I wondered, *How can we take Indian pastors from all over, bring them together, and then maximize our efforts?* I started jotting down notes. One of those was this: We've got to do something like this with church planting.

When I returned home, we had our first pastor's conference. Everything was in the Tamil language. For two more years, our conferences were also in Tamil, but by the fourth year, we had people coming from other states, so we had to have translators. At that point, we started forming smaller groups in various regions, and that was when we started talking about regional network groups. It was then that I knew that the future of our movement lay in those regional networks. They were the backbone of everything that we did. The networks became the mechanism to bring training in the word, fellowship, and accountability in the midst of great diversity.

While inspired by the airline alliances of the late '80s, of course, our networks are very different. If I had to choose the most outstanding difference, I'd say it is that our networks are deeply relational. Relationships are the connective tissue. Accountability is relational— it's not administrative; reporting is relational—workers share information with each other, rather than only getting it "top down"; resource generation and distribution is relational—the people on the field and living in the villages tell us what their needs are; we don't inform them of what their needs are.

Our networks are structured in such a way that they encourage people to make their own choices and decisions based on their own context. This approach is different from someone in an office "directing" others from the top down. Our networks give great access to training and equipping. Rather than asking workers and leaders to give up weeks at a time to travel across the country for training that may or may not connect with their culture, we equip them at the grassroots level in a very contextual and relevant way.

Equipping large, decentralized groups inside an "unchanging and flexible" model has its challenges, but we're excited about how the Lord has led us here. Each year, our leadership prayerfully considers a theme in scripture that will build a foundation of knowledge for the thousands of pastors and workers in our network. For instance, in the past couple years, we've studied "The Church" and "Prayer." We create a broad outline, full of scripture, and then we gather people in local conferences to teach that theme. Each of those people, then, is responsible to take what they've learned back to their own village and share it with their circle.

Our approach to training has both challenges and opportunities. If we were to write up an entire script and then tell people to translate it and teach it word for word, the unchanging core of truth would likely not be contextualized well. Of course, there's danger in how scripture is interpreted, so through relationships, accountability, and discipleship we seek to equip all people to accurately handle the word of truth. This danger, however, doesn't keep us from putting the word of God into the hands of the people. We believe in leaving significant room for the Holy Spirit to do his work. We are trusting God's word to speak and the Holy Spirit to do his work.

Praise the Lord that over thirty years ago, the Lord impressed these principles upon us. He showed us the value in structures that deliver an unchanging core—the message of the gospel—inside a flexible skin. Because of our robust, relational networks, we have an infrastructure that is easy to grow and replicate, ready to support church planting, discipleship, and saturating in diverse cultures throughout the villages of India. I would say that this is a significant provision that has led to the remarkable growth we are experiencing today.

Saturating Churches Are . . .

. . . Life-giving

I think we know that the word *church* is not ever used to describe a building in the New Testament. Not once. Even though we know this full well, believers have continued to dedicate immense energy, resources, and prideful identification with brick and mortar buildings that are used to house the people of God once a week.

God has described the true church in a variety of ways, and from all kinds of angles, to help us round out our view of this relational, in-motion, organic, human and spiritual thing that is his church. It's called the *ecclesia*, which is the assembly or the gathering of believers. It's the *oikos*, the household of God. It's *koinonia*, the fellowship of believers. It is called the temple. The household of God. The bride of Christ. The body of Christ.

From the launching pad of the local church, the body of Christ is the incarnate presence of Christ in this world. And what does Jesus do? If he were walking the face of the earth today, he would be doing the same things he did as described on the pages of the gospel narratives: bringing life. Jesus said, "I am the life. I came to give life. I came to bring abundant life" (John 10:10). So if the church is indeed the body of Christ, then the church is what God uses today to bring life! Its mission is to bring life, to rejuvenate whatever is dead in the community, to find what is lost, to refresh what is withering around it. God is not going to wave a magic wand in order to bring life. He has chosen to do it through us, the Church. He has invited us to be image bearers, life-givers, and redeemers. If the church doesn't fulfill that responsibility, it doesn't fulfill its mission.

Our Indian "barefoot pastors" go into a village, leading with the gospel. They introduce Jesus, the one true God, who came so that all people everywhere can be forgiven, reconciled, adopted, and justified. As people in that village put their trust in Jesus, a village church is formed. That church, then, has a responsibility for bringing life in every dimension and aspect—spiritual, social, ethical, moral, and physical.

In the first part of John 10:10, Jesus says that the enemy

comes to steal, kill, and destroy. It is our enemy who has taken health and life from the community and replaced it with darkness, ignorance, poverty, superstitious beliefs and practices, illness, disharmony, fragmentation, jealousy, and hatred. When a gospel-first church is planted in a community, it gradually removes all of that! The body of Christ brings real life into that village—the abundant life that Jesus came to give. So if a church is not aware of that mission, or is not equipped to fulfill that mission, then in essence, it is not a church! It may be a very nice social club or a safe enclave or a place to experience a comforting routine, but it is not be the life force that Jesus intended it to be.

It seems to me that Western-style, institutional churches have focused most on one aspect of the Church—the household of God—and forgotten that the church is more than that.

The church loses its ability to influence and impact the village or the community when it doesn't see itself holistically, as described in scripture. The church is to be the very presence of Jesus Christ in its community. It is the fresh breath of life through which people experience the compassion of Christ and the truth of his character! I am convinced that God's chosen way of bringing life to a community is through the body of Christ.

. . . Reproducing

Obviously, healthy, reproducing churches are at the center of our strategy to saturate communities and regions with the gospel. But why? What is the basis? Let's look to God's word for the answer:

> Jesus also said, "The Kingdom of God is like a farmer who scatters seed on the ground. Night and day, while he's asleep or awake, the seed sprouts and grows, but he does not understand how it happens. The earth produces the crops on its own. First a leaf blade pushes through, then the heads of wheat are formed, and finally the grain ripens. And as soon

as the grain is ready, the farmer comes and harvests it with a sickle, for the harvest time has come." (Mark 4:26–29 NLT)

Seeds have within their DNA the capacity to reproduce and replicate themselves. When you plant a seed, it automatically grows, reproduces, and multiplies. Similarly, new-life Christ followers have within themselves the capacity to "do his will" and to please God!

> Now may the God of peace—
> who brought up from the dead our Lord Jesus,
> the great Shepherd of the sheep,
> and ratified an eternal covenant with his blood—
> may he equip you with all you need
> for doing his will.
> May he produce in you,
> through the power of Jesus Christ,
> every good thing that is pleasing to him.
> All glory to him forever and ever! Amen.
>
> (Hebrews 13:20–21 NLT)

God has put this capacity into our spiritual DNA! The church, made up of equipped believers, has also been given gifts: apostles, prophets, evangelists, pastors, and teachers (Ephesians 4:11). It is at the core of who we are to grow and reproduce, night and day, whether the farmer is asleep or awake. This is who we are, but how is it that so many churches are not living out who they were made to be?

When a church is not reproducing, I believe it's often because we have put certain controls or a damper on our innate ability to grow and multiply. Confining organic, reproducing life under the strictures of tradition, rules, and culture certainly stifles growth. And yet too many continue to create barriers to growth based on "who is allowed to do what." Only seminary-trained pastors can teach the Bible. Serving is limited to "being a greeter" or "collecting the offering." As long as this is so, how will we ever unleash Holy Spirit-filled believers to do the significant work God has equipped them for and placed before them?

How will we ever unleash the church?

If we want a harvest, we need to remove the barriers that box in growth. Let's pull back the barriers, and watch the sprouts push through, the heads of wheat form, the grain ripen—and then let's be ready to gather in the harvest of the reproducing church.

. . . A Sustainable Witness

A church creates a sustainable witness in only one way: through discipleship. In 2 Timothy 2:2, Paul says, "And what you have heard from me in the presence of many witnesses entrust to faithful men, who will be able to teach others also" (ESV). This entrusting of life and passing on of life is what keeps a movement moving. When relational, life-on-life, rooted-in-the-word discipleship is happening in the church, then that church stays vital, energized, and alive!

Imagine if believers were individually and corporately searching the scriptures, depending on the Spirit, exercising their gifts, and bringing life to their community. Would they be dependent on a governing structure? No! Would they be dependent on big money? No! Would they need to look elsewhere to hire a teaching pastor or someone gifted in administration or someone to reach youth? No! Each local church is unique, and each certainly has its own strengths and weaknesses, but when the local body of Christ is full of people who are taking their places in it, it is equipped enough to do what the Lord has put in front of it.

Every level of what we do in IGL is designed to be sustainable. We are not interested in creating dependency. We believe deeply in the dignity of God's creation—and in each person's and community's abilities to contribute and to grow. While a cornerstone of what we do is to support pastors and new churches, we do this in a way that sets them up for success and to be self-sustaining. Barefoot pastors, for example, receive support for only two years and villages receive support for five. At the end of that five-year period, a village should have holistic assets that allow it to flourish: a new Life Center (or community center), a clean water well, a school, job training, skills training, and perhaps a daycare. And at the center of it all is the life-giving force of the growing body of Christ.

ACHIEVE 2040

A church in every village by 2040. This is possible. We have the relational infrastructure through discipleship and through regional networks. Our churches are life-giving and reproducing. Our pastors and workers are excited, energized, and committed. Most importantly, God is working. The blind see, the lame walk, those in darkness have seen a great light. The Holy Spirit is igniting hearts for Jesus Christ in India. What a privilege it is to play even a small part in this work of God today.

REFLECT

1. In 1996, IGL set a goal to reach 1,000 villages by the year 2020. They reached 20,000 instead. To date, there are churches in 250,000 villages! Many of us have experienced this powerful God as he is described in Ephesians 3:20. "…[He] is able to do immeasurably more than all we ask or imagine, according to his power that is at work within us…" (NIV). What has God's leading led you to do in your local fellowship?

2. There are 600,000 villages in India with 1,600–1,800 people groups amongst them. ACHIEVE 2040 is a bold vision to reach all 600,000 by the year 2040. This seems like a tall order, but Colossians 1:3–4, 6 says:

   > We always pray for you, and we give thanks to God, the Father of our Lord Jesus Christ. For we have heard of your faith in Christ Jesus and your love for all of God's people . . . This same Good News that came to you is going out all over the world. It is bearing fruit everywhere by changing lives, just as it changed your lives from the day you first heard and understood the truth about God's wonderful grace. (NLT)

Would you participate in accomplishing this bold goal by praying regularly and asking some of your friends to join in with you? What other ways might God be asking you to participate?

3. Consider Pastor Rao's experience: he was beaten and driven out of a village. But his burden and prayer for those people only intensified. Eventually, his abusers sought him out to apologize, and almost all the families in the village put their trust in Jesus. They were transformed from living like savages to becoming a resource for surrounding villages through the Adopt A Village program. Have you had an experience (perhaps less dramatic) where you were rejected as you shared the gospel? How have you responded to that rejection? In the face of it, how has the Lord led you?

CHALLENGE

1. Relationally based, saturating church growth should be something we can see anywhere, through discipleship and effective equipping. The principles described in this chapter result in multiplication of churches rather than in just adding one church plant at a time. What does equipping look like in your church? How is relational discipleship happening? What are ways you see workers being equipped?

2. It's refreshing to think about the way seeds grow, fueled by the replicating DNA inside them, according to Mark 4:26–29:

> Jesus also said, "The Kingdom of God is like a farmer who scatters seed on the ground. Night and day, while he's asleep or awake, the seed sprouts and grows, but he does not understand how it happens. The earth produces the crops on its own. First a leaf blade pushes through, then the heads of wheat are formed, and finally the grain ripens. And as soon as the grain is ready, the farmer comes and harvests it with a sickle, for the harvest time has come." (NLT)

This book suggests that if a church of equipped believers is not reproducing, it may be because it is imposing controls that damper the natural growth of a seed. These controls may be "strictures of tradition, rules, and culture." For instance: only seminary trained pastors can teach the Bible; serving is narrowly defined and is limited to small roles such as collecting the offering. What controls seem familiar in your situation? What other ways might "the seed" be boxed in but could be released to grow?

KINGDOM VOICES

Steve Moore
Former Executive Director of Missio Nexus, Executive Director of nexleader

There are some very compelling voices, Francis Chan being one of them, who are suggesting that our traditional Western models of church actually create structures that make it harder for us to develop disciples who flourish in the use of their gifts. And part of that problem is that the structures we've created call for a professionalized ministry, with college-trained, if not seminary-trained, leaders. I'm not opposed to education, by any means, but one of the things that I hear as well is that bi-vocational church leadership doesn't work because leaders can't do a job and take on the leadership role of a church at the same time as that church grows.

There's probably some truth to that in the framework of professionalized ministry, but if the goal is not to grow the church to two hundred people but to stop whenever you get to thirty or forty people and reproduce another group, then you could actually have people who are bi-vocational who are providing meaningful, thoughtful, Jesus-focused, discipleship leadership to a group of twenty-five or thirty people and also working a full-time job. But because our paradigm for the preferred models of church require it to be large in order to support a professionalized staff, we can't see that. Francis Chan is one of the really loud voices on this.

And what if we actually had a network of churches who didn't own any property? What if these churches were pastored by bi-vocational leaders who multiplied every time they grew beyond a certain capacity? Then we could continue to do that. The problem is, we would look at that mentality in China or in India or in Indonesia, and we would say it's brilliant. But when somebody suggests that we should be thinking about it in Western culture, there's a fairly significant amount of pushback.

chapter 11

JOIN THE WORK: GIVE AND GROW

Chapter 11
Join the Work: Give and Grow

Over the years, I've gotten to know many of you. I've gotten to know your people, your churches. I know that even as the culture is lapping at the doors, your heart's desire is to take the gospel out and see it transform the lives of your people, your neighbors, and your communities. I know that although we are over 8,000 miles apart, your hearts are with us as we move out across India, taking the hope of Jesus to those who have never heard.

Let's join hands in the work. In God's work.

Long ago, when I was a much younger man, one of the first Western churches I ever visited was a brand-new, tiny group of people who were meeting in a strip mall storefront. Eight families had come together to plant this community, which they called Hope Community Church. The pastor, Steve, was twenty-nine years old, and although he showed up to lead, he wasn't sure that he was up for the task of leading and growing this little group. He worried about his youth and his inexperience in preparing teachings regularly.

Despite his youth and inexperience, God had given Steve a clear vision for this group. He and I were talking about it recently, and he said, "It's easy when you plant a church. From the jump, you build it around values that are close to God's heart." Church plants or not, Steve said, "Leaders need to lead the way, make a push, and start talking early and often about God's heart for the lost. All the lost. They need to teach that his direction is GO."

From their very first year, Hope Community Church got involved in investing in our work in India. Of course, their finances were tight and stretched. They were a small group, growing with new believers and young people. Still, they were committed to giving and emphasized stewarding their resources. "I believe God blessed that," Steve said. They were faithful with a little, and so God entrusted them with more.

That is his way.

How were they blessed? Well, despite small means, they never missed a bill. God always provided. Steve told me, "You might think that because resources were tight that we'd need to hold back or wait until it made more 'sense' to start investing outside our local church, but we really wanted to be part of the big work that God was doing."

They are still serious about investing in God's work. God has blessed them with the ability to "never miss a bill," but even more significantly, he's given them fruit. Today they've seen over 1,000 salvations and are a church of 1,000 regular members. The "fruit" is fruitful—these people have the DNA of outward focus and sacrificial giving. This church, even when it "couldn't," chose to invest in the Kingdom, to work where God is working, and has now been blessed to give at a much larger scale.

What a privilege it has been for them to see the opportunity and to step into it. To be part of something so much bigger than their own group.

I fervently believe that discouraged Western churches can be encouraged, revitalized, and re-energized as they partner in the big work God is doing in India. It's a thrill. It's an adventure. It's a joy. Most of all, it is where God is working, and it has vast eternal significance.

It's no surprise that when people are engaged, encouraged, and re-energized around significant spiritual work, energy builds. It grows and is channeled into even more areas where God is working. As you lead your people toward outward focus—to go and give—you will see them grow. You will see them become fruitful and significant in ways that you couldn't have imagined. God will unleash the willing church and invite them to work where he is working.

Of course, you can do God's amazing work in your community. I hope this book spurs you on to grow and multiply. But I also invite you to partner with us. I'm going to outline ways that you can join this work and lead your fellowship in the direction of GO.

1. Go to our website (iglworld.org) and learn more about what India Gospel League is doing in South Asia. Understanding what God

is doing will help you pray more effectively.

2. Pray. Please don't overlook this way of partnering with us or skim past it. Matthew 6:21 says, "For where your treasure is, there your heart will be also" (NIV). Certainly, we often think about this in the context of money. But it applies generally to an investment. Investing in prayer is the most powerful way to steer the direction of our hearts to God's heart. When you pray for the work in India, we are co-laborers working inside of God's will, joining together to ask the Lord of the Harvest to send workers into the fields. We benefit so much from your partnership in this way. We are sustained, encouraged, protected, and provided for. Please pray.

Here are things you can pray for:

- Pray for people to be disappointed in their false gods and religions and turn to the one true God. (Jeremiah 2:28)
- Pray for "people of peace" who will receive those bringing the gospel and be bridges to others in their communities. (Psalm 41:2)
- Pray against oppression, and pray for courage and wisdom for believers facing oppression. (Psalm 72:13)
- Pray for protection for workers in the northern part of India specifically and that the gospel message would go out undeterred. (Psalm 91:14–15)
- Pray that God will use his people to deliver the gospel message to every one of the 600,000 villages in India by 2040. (Psalm 96:3)

1. Go (Come, See, Serve). For years, we've invited people to visit us in India. We want you to come and see what God is doing. You can visit Sharon Campus, spend time with the children here, visit the schools, tour the hospital, and eat meals with us. Of course, we might put you to work teaching the Bible as well. Our people are delighted and feel so "seen" when brothers and sisters from across the world come to their churches. And they love to hear what you have to say about your life and Jesus

in your life. The children love it when you share your story, and especially when you do a dance for them. (Even if it's bad dancing, they love it!)

Other ways to come, see, and serve are through our medical and veterinary visiting teams. These teams help provide for people living in villages where dental care, vision care, and other needs are not readily acquired.

We also invite you to help equip the thousands of young leaders who are being raised up to serve. If you are a Bible teacher or a pastor, we'd love for you and a team to join us at a regional training conference. We'll communicate our theme to you, and through a translator, you can help prepare these eager young believers to go out to their people with the gospel!

2. Give. It is deeply important to us that our indigenous ministries be self-sustaining, and that value is woven into everything that we do. At the same time, as a ministry among the poorest of the poor, we use seed money to prepare the way for self-sustaining work. I've come to believe (and observe) that God delights in moving resources around. He, after all, is the owner of the cattle on a thousand hills. I think he loves inviting his children who are stewarding more "cattle" to share them with those who have fewer.

While giving money may sometimes seem difficult (and for some it certainly is a difficulty), there is almost no quicker and more practical way to say to God, "I trust you to provide for me, and I trust you to use what I give for eternal purposes." When we give, we accept God's invitation to participate in his exciting work.

Check out our website for all the ways you can partner with us in this work, from building a well, supporting a barefoot pastor, sponsoring a child, to providing a micro-loan and many more. You can even rally as a small group or church community to "adopt" a village, which provides the local village church resources to share the gospel and holistically bless its neighbors. As with our other programs, adopting a village is a limited commitment. In this case, it is five years. In five years, we expect to see adopted churches and their community efforts become self-sustaining, self-supporting, self-governing, and self-replicating.

3. Tell. God is doing something big in India, but it seems that not many people know about it. We'd like to see all 600,000 villages in India reached by the gospel by 2040, but perhaps we should also have a goal that every American church is aware of this great opportunity! Help us get the word out. Pray for us in your churches, tell your friends, get creative (with a Punjab Prom or Basketball for Bibles)! God is doing great things in India, and we want to give more people a chance to be part of it!

There is no greater joy in my life than following Jesus and inviting others to come along. I remain stunned and grateful that the Lord has positioned me to introduce Jesus and his message of hope to millions who are living in darkness. Join me in this joy. Join me in this opportunity. Work where God is working. Grow through giving.

> *How beautiful on the mountains are the feet of those who bring good news, who proclaim peace, who bring good tidings, who proclaim salvation, who say to Zion, "Your God reigns!" (Isaiah 52:7 NIV).*

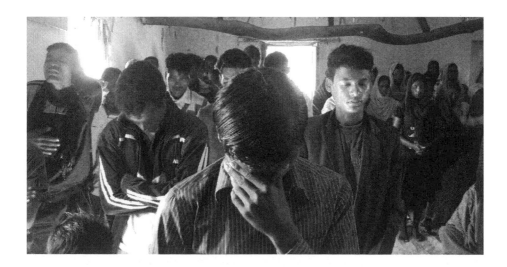

Acknowledgments

Many friends—dear brothers and sisters—came together to help with this book. Not unlike God's work in India, he brought together precious members of the body of Christ to join in the work.

Particularly, I'd like to thank all of the people that were interviewed—in the States and in India. Their insights and perspectives were invaluable, and even beyond what you see printed here, their words and ideas informed this material. Thank you to Jim Lyon, Warren Bird, Dave Ferguson, Steve Moore, Steve Weldon, Reggie McNeal, Rebecca Stanley, Gary Kinnaman, Paul Cornelius, Selvasingh Watson, and Reverend Vasanthraj.

It was a joy to interview some of my friends near Sharon Campus. They provided important, firsthand descriptions of what it looks like to come to Christ out of a Hindu background. I'm grateful for the time these brothers and sisters took to speak with me, as well as for their openness about their lives. Thank you to Stephen, R. Shanthi, and Dayal.

It was wonderful to work with folks from Freedom Fellowship in Northeast Ohio. Thank you to Andie, Neil, and Erin for sharing your stories and to Kathryn, Lina, Alex, Elli, and Indre for working with me to create the end of chapter questions.

Much gratitude to my assistant in India, Vanitha. She knows my schedule better than I do and has an incredible ability to access information and disseminate it in an instant. Thank you, Mallory in the US office, for managing this project.

My wife, as always, deserves a huge thanks. She is a powerful servant of the Lord, and her unwavering partnership with me in India Gospel League is both an inspiration and a strong foundation.

I saved the best for last. Mere words cannot express the immense gratitude I feel in my heart for Heidi Muller. Without your help and sacrifice, this book would have never seen the light of day. Thank you. You walked more than the 'second mile' on this journey with me.

My gratitude to the Lord overflows. He is my source and my goal. I am eternally indebted to him both for my salvation and for his allowance to participate in his great work.

About the Author

Samuel Stephens is a pastor, speaker, author, and the president of India Gospel League (IGL), an indigenous mission agency headquartered in Salem, Tamil Nadu, South India.

He graduated with a bachelor's degree in arts from the Madras University in 1973. He did his post-graduate theological studies in missions at the Union Biblical Seminary in Central India and graduated in 1977 from the Serampore University with a degree in divinity. He also received his doctor of ministry in leadership and global perspectives from George Fox University.

Samuel joined the ministry in 1976 as a barefoot pastor. In 1988, shortly after the death of his father, Sam took over as president of IGL. Though he had learned much on the field and was being groomed to take the helm, he wondered if he was really ready. By God's grace, he moved IGL forward, establishing international support as well as a new vision. As he states in his book *The Kairos Moment*: "Now is the time. We need to see the world with a Kingdom perspective. I'm speaking of God's vision for every culture, tongue, and tribe in my country and around the world."

It has been under Sam's leadership that unprecedented and substantial growth has happened with up to 100,000 new churches planted in India since 1992. That growth continues to explode and multiply.

Not only is Sam president of IGL, but he passionately plays the role of entrepreneur and founder of other establishments, as he is committed to transforming the lives and living conditions of people in rural villages.

Sam and his wife Prati have nine children (seven of them adopted). The home that he shares with his wife is home to a larger family of 400 orphans. Where most CEOs may have a swimming pool or tennis court in the backyard, Sam has built a community college, a cancer center and hospital, and multiple other facilities, including a print shop and coffee plantation—all of which provide employment and the highest level of service to the poorest of the poor. Sam also started *Jeevan Sahaya Nidhi* (The Life Fund), a micro-credit program that empowers thousands of rural women.

It is worth noting that the Sharon Cancer Center and General Hospital, which he established, is one of the very few cancer centers in the country, providing preventative and quality medical care to the rural population in the district. The hospital also carries out community health programs through mobile medical camps. Sam also serves as the managing trustee of the Sharon Palliative Care Center, also based in Salem.

Sam is founder and president of the Non-Denominational Association of Interdependent Churches (NAIC), an organization that unites more than 35,000 indigenous churches throughout India. He is also the founder and president of the Association of Indigenous Ministries that enables more than 300 indigenous Christian organizations in the country to work together for the highest good.

And in the few spare minutes of his day, Sam has served as honorary president of the Asia and Pacific Alliance of YMCAs as well as the Deputy President of the World Alliance of YMCAs. He's also part of the local Rotary Club in Salem and has developed several key programs with Rotary International.

Occasionally he sits back and enjoys a good chai tea and time with his many grandchildren.

Notes

End Notes

[1] *Lion*. Directed by Garth Davis. Sydney: See Saw Films, 2016.

[2] Rod Dreher, "Orthodox Christians Must Now Learn to Live as Exiles in Our Own Country," *Time Magazine*, June 26, 2015, https://time.com/3938050/orthodox-christians-must-now-learn-to-live-as-exiles-in-our-own-country/.

[3] Dr. Richard J. Krejcir, "Statistics and Reasons for Church Decline," Church Leadership, accessed November 4, 2019, http://www.churchleadership.org/apps/articles/default.asp?articleid=42346.

[4] The Barna Group, "Almost Half of Practicing Christian Millennials Say Evangelism Is Wrong," Barna Group, February 5, 2019, https://www.barna.com/research/millennials-oppose-evangelism/.

[5] Sarah Eekhoff Zylstra, "What Millennials Really Think About Evangelism," The Gospel Coalition, February 28,2019, https://www.thegospelcoalition.org/article/millennials-really-think-evangelism/.

[6] Jack Jenkins, "'Nones' now as big as evangelicals, Catholics in the US," Religion News Service, March 21,2019, https://religionnews.com/2019/03/21/nones-now-as-big-as-evangelicals-catholics-in-the-us/.

[7] Ryan P. Burge, "Evangelicals Show No Decline Despite Trump and 'Nones,'" March 21, 2019, https://www.christianitytoday.com/news/2019/march/evangelical-nones-mainline-us-general-social-survey-gss.html.

[8] Jack Jenkins, "'Nones' now as big as evangelicals, Catholics in the US," Religion News Service, March 21,2019, https://religionnews.com/2019/03/21/nones-now-as-big-as-evangelicals-catholics-in-the-us/.

[9] Ryan P. Burge, "Evangelicals Show No Decline Despite Trump and 'Nones,'" March 21, 2019, https://www.christianitytoday.com/news/2019/march/evangelical-nones-mainline-us-general-social-survey-gss.html.

[10] The Barna Group, "The State of the Church 2016," Barna Group, September 15, 2016, https://www.barna.com/research/state-church-2016/.

[11] Open Doors, "World Watch List," Open Doors USA, Accessed August 5, 2019, https://www.opendoorsusa.org/christian-persecution/world-watch-list/.

[12] John Stott, *Basic Christianity*, New Edition (Downers Grove, Il: InterVarsity Press, 2008).

[13] The Barna Group, "The State of the Church 2016," Barna Group, September 15, 2016, https://www.barna.com/research/state-church-2016/.

[14] The Barna Group, "Americans Divided on the Importance of Church," Barna Group, March 24, 2014, https://www.barna.com/research/americans-divided-on-the-importance-of-church/#.V-hxhLVy6FD.

[15] The Barna Group, "Almost Half of Practicing Christian Millennials Say Evangelism Is Wrong," Barna Group, February 5, 2019, https://www.barna.com/research/millennials-oppose-evangelism/.

[16] The Barna Group, "Six Reasons Young Christians Leave Church," Barna Group, September 27, 2011, https://www.barna.com/research/six-reasons-young-christians-leave-church/.

[17] Aaron Earls, "Most Teenagers Drop Out of Church as Young Adults," LifeWay Research, January 15, 2019, https://lifewayresearch.com/2019/01/15/most-teenagers-drop-out-of-church-as-young-adults/.

[18] Daniel Yankelovich, *New Rules: Searching for Self-Fulfillment in a World Turned Upside Down*. (New York: Random House, 1981), 242.

[19] Thom S. Rainer, "Hope for Dying Churches," LifeWay, January 16, 2018, https://factsandtrends.net/2018/01/16/hope-for-dying-churches/.

[20] 75 percent of the world's Christians now live outside of North American and Western Europe, making African and Eastern countries the new locus for Christianity.

[21] "Evangelical Growth," Operation World, Accessed August 28, 2019, http://www.operationworld.org/hidden/evangelical-growth.

[22] Ibid.

[23] "Evangelical Population," Operation World, Accessed August 28, 2019, http://www.operationworld.org/hidden/evangelical-population.

[24] "India," Operation World, Accessed August 28, 2019, http://www.operationworld.org/country/indi/owtext.html.

[25] We are supposing that all believers have a role to play in the body of Christ, and we use the term "workers" to describe every believer who is taking up his or her role.

[26] Energy World, "World's Top 10 Countries in Wind Energy Capacity," *Economic Times*, March 18, 2019, https://energy.economictimes.indiatimes.com/news/renewable/worlds-top-10-countries-in-wind-energy-capacity/68465090.

[27] Mridul Chadha, "India's Wind Capacity Crosses 10% Share in Overall Installed Base," CleanTechnica, January 21, 2019, https://cleantechnica.com/2019/01/21/indias-wind-capacity-crosses-10-share-in-overall-installed-base/.

[28] "Electricity," US Energy Information Administration, accessed August 27, 2019, https://www.eia.gov/electricity/monthly/.

[29] As a pushback against the syncretistic, pantheistic worldview in India, we ask that before new believers are baptized, they share the gospel message with at least two other people and bring them to the Lord. This is not a biblical requirement, of course, but in our cultural context, it helps to ensure that people understand the exclusive and personal claims of the gospel, are able to articulate them, and are willing to share their faith. As a result, each new believer often brings two disciples along to witness and celebrate their testimony and baptism.

[30] Brett Miller, "Do Western Missionaries Damage Cultures?" TEAM accessed August 3, 2019, https://team.org/blog/do-western-missionaries-damage-cultures.

[31] Cyril Bruce Firth, *An Introduction to Indian Church History* (Madras, India: Published for the Senate of Serampore College by ISPCK, 1968), 3–6.

[32] David Barret, ed., *World Christian Encyclopedia*, vol. 1(New York: Oxford University Press, 1982), 373.

33 Francis Thonippara, "St. Thomas Christians: The First Indigenous Church of India" in *Christianity is Indian: The Emergence of an Indigenous Community*, ed. Roger E. Hedlund (Delhi: Published for MIIS, Mylapore by ISPCK, 2000), 63.

34 Antony Mathias Mundadan, *History of Christianity in India. Vol.1* (Bangalore: Theological Publ. of India, 1984), 36–38.

35 Ibid, 78.

36 Ibid, 36–38.

37 Francis Thonippara, "The First Indigenous Church of India: *St. Thomas Christians*," in *Christianity is Indian: The Emergence of an Indigenous Community*, ed. Roger E. Hedlund (Delhi: Published for MIIS, Mylapore by ISPCK, 2000), 71–75.

38 Vishal Mangalwadi, *The Legacy of William Carey: A Model for the Transformation of a Culture* (Wheaton, IL: Crossway Books, 1999), 24–25.

39 Sunil Kumar Chartterjee, "Pioneers of Indigeneity in Bengal," in *Christianity is Indian: The Emergence of an Indigenous Community*, ed. Roger E. Hedlund (Delhi: Published for MIIS, Mylapore by ISPCK, 2000), 182.

40 Costi W. Hinn, "3 Takeaways from India 2019," For the Gospel, February 6, 2019, http://www.forthegospel.org/3-takeaways-from-india-2019/.

41 Thomson Reuters Foundation, "Thomson Reuters Foundation Annual Poll: The World's Most Dangerous Countries for Women, 2018," Accessed August 5, 2019, http://poll2018.trust.org/.

42 Matt Smethurst, "The Subtle Danger of Mission Drift," The Gospel Coalition, March 10, 2014, https://www.thegospelcoalition.org/article/the-subtle-danger-of-mission-drift/.

43 "History of Indian Telecommunication," *Telecom Talk*, March 29, 2011, https://telecomtalk.info/history-of-indian-telecommunication/67789/.

44 "Telecom Industry in India," *India Brand Equity Foundation*, July 2019, https://www.ibef.org/industry/telecommunications.aspx.

45 Ibid.

46 Shubham Agarwal, "WhatsApp has 400 million users in India, but no fix for its fake news problem," Digital Trends, August 12, 2019, https://www.digitaltrends.com/news/whatsapp-india-fake-news-lynchings/.

47 Sasha Ingber and Lauren Frayer, "Modi Wins in Landslide Election, a Victory for Hindu Nationalists," NPR, May 23, 2019, https://www.npr.org/2019/05/23/726160387/modi-wins-in-landslide-election-a-victory-for-hindu-nationalists.

48 Temple, James. "India's Water Crisis Is Already Here," *MITTechnology Review*, April 24, 2019, https://www.technologyreview.com/s/613344/indias-water-crisis-is-already-here-climate-change-will-compound-it/.

49 Awasthy, Aayushi. "Why India needs to worry about climate change," *BBC News*, British Broadcasting Association, October 25, 2018, https://www.bbc.com/news/world-asia-india-45949323.

50 Eusebius, *The Church History*, trans. Paul L. Meier (Grand Rapids: Kregel, 2007), 293. In other editions, see IX.viii.13–15.

51 Julian, "Fragment of a Letter to a Priest," in *The Works of the Emperor Julian*, vol. 2, trans. Wilmer Cave Wright (New York: MacMillan, 1913), 337.

52 Krishnavatar Sharma, "India Has 139 Internal Migrants," World Economic Forum, October 1, 2017, https://www.weforum.org/agenda/2017/10/india-has-139-million-internal-migrants-we-must-not-forget-them/.

53 Cornelis Bennema and Paul Joshua Bhakiaraj, eds., *Indian and Christian: Changing Identities in Modern India:Papers from the First SAIACS Annual Consultation* (Bangalore: SAIACS Press, 2011), 8–12.

54 Ann Voskamp, *The Broken Way* (Grand Rapids: Zondervan, 2016), 69.

55 "India Population 2019," World Population Review, accessed October 27, 2019, http://worldpopulationreview.com/countries/india-population/.

56 "United States Population 2019," World Population Review, accessed October 27, 2019, http://worldpopulationreview.com/countries/united-states-population/.

[57] "Country: India," Joshua Project, accessed October 25, 2019, https://joshuaproject.net/countries/IN.

[58] Ibid.

[59] Richa Verma, "600,000 or 1 million? India unclear on its village count, and why that matters," Business Standard, August 14, 2017, https://www.business-standard.com/article/current-affairs/600-000-or-1-million-india-unclear-on-its-village-count-why-that-matters-117080300287_1.html.

[60] "Religion," Census India, accessed October 25, 2019, http://censusindia.gov.in/Census_And_You/religion.aspx.

[61] Soutik Biswas, "The Man Who 'Discovered' 780 Indian Languages," BBC News, October 17, 2017, https://www.bbc.com/news/world-asia-india-41718082.

[62] "World Watch List: India," Open Doors USA, accessed October 25, 2019, https://www.opendoorsusa.org/christian-persecution/world-watch-list/india/.

[63] "India's Poverty Profile," The World Bank, accessed October 29, 2019, https://www.worldbank.org/en/news/infographic/2016/05/27/india-s-poverty-profile.

[64] "Crimes Against Women Have Gone Up 200% Since 1995," *The Times of India*, May 6, 2017, https://timesofindia.indiatimes.com/india/crimes-against-women-have-gone-up-200-since-1995/articleshow/58546654.cms.

[65] Water Aid, "India Ranked First in the World for Most Rural People Without Access to Clean Water," March 21, 2017, https://www.wateraidindia.in/fr/node/3956.

[66] Vibhuti Agarwal, "Indians Have the Worst Access to Safe Drinking Water in the World," March 22, 2016, https://blogs.wsj.com/indiarealtime/2016/03/22/indians-have-the-worst-access-to-safe-drinking-water-in-the-world/.

[67] Isha Chakraborty, "Rural Healthcare Structure, A Challenge Yet to be Resolved," Business Economics, July 2, 2018, http://businesseconomics.in/rural-healthcare-sector-challenge-yet-be-resolved.

Share *Unleashed* on social!

IGLWorld.org / 888.352.4451

Contact IGL to receive updates or find out
how you and your church can join us in the work
that God is doing in India.